KEITH WITHNALL

CW00370124

CareerTracking

The 26
Success Shortcuts
to the Top

To our mothers, Jeanne and Loretta

CareerTracking

The 26
Success Shortcuts
to the Top

Jimmy Calano
Jeff Salzman

Gower

© Jimmy Calano and Jeff Salzman 1988

All rights reserved. No part of this publication may be reproduced, stored in a retrieval system, or transmitted in any form or by any means, electronic, mechanical, photocopying, recording, or otherwise without the prior permission of Wildwood House Limited.

First published in North America by Simon & Schuster Inc, 1988.

This edition published in the UK by
Gower Publishing Company Ltd
Gower House
Croft Road
Aldershot
Hants GU11 3HR
England

British Library Cataloguing in Publication Data

Calano, Jimmy
    Careertracking: 26 success shortcuts to
    the top.
    1. Careers. Development
    I. Title II. Salzman, Jeff
    33.17'02

Hardback ISBN 0 7045 3104 6
Paperback ISBN 0 7045 0598 3

Typeset in Great Britain by
Guildford Graphics Limited, Petworth, West Sussex
Printed and bound in Great Britain by
Billing & Sons Ltd, Worcester

CONTENTS

ACKNOWLEDGEMENTS

We wish to thank the following people for helping us make this book happen:

Ed Bliss, one of our top trainers, for his editorial input and tweaks.

John Boswell, our literary agent, for his ideas and expertise.

Vic Conant and Dave Nightingale, for putting our words on tape.

Delynn Copley, our marketing whiz kid, for helping us brainstorm and write the very first *Success Shortcuts* pamphlet.

Teresa Goodwin and Diane Lewis, our proofreaders, for dotting our i's and crossing our t's. Kimberley Ruhe and Leslie Allen our copy editors, for making our writing square with the rules (most of them, anyway).

Fred Hills, our editor, for believing in the book and giving it a title.

Andrea Meyer, our researcher, for checking every last fact.

Bob Purcell, our attorney, for keeping us on the right side of the law.

T. Robert Taylor, Anne Vaughan, Marian McCanless, Carol Frietsch and our art team, for their endless patience.

Our heroes, Ken Blanchard, Wayne Dyer, Harold Geneen, and Tom Peters, for inspiring us.

Our employees, for trying our ideas and following our lead.

Our families, for their support and encouragement.

Our special friends (you know who you are), for hanging in there while we were busy writing.

Our seminar participants, for teaching us as much as we hope we have taught them.

The Two Big Questions

Question 1: What Does It Really Take to Be Successful?

After helping over a million professionals reach their career goals through our company, CareerTrack, we think we know.

We have identified the twenty-six skills (we call them Success Shortcuts) that we believe constitute the difference between 'making it' and 'making it big'. They have been tested in the only place that counts — the business world. *CareerTracking* deals with each of these skills, one to a chapter.

The purpose of *CareerTracking* is to distil success knowledge to its essence and present it in a way that you can digest easily and put to work efficiently. *Efficiently* is the key word here. If there's one standard complaint we hear from virtually every professional we work with, it's 'I don't have enough time' — which is simply another way of saying, 'I have too much work'. Today, long hours at the office are not just for workaholics; heavy workloads have become the norm. And as competitiveness continues to increase into the 1990s, no relief is in sight.

Yet, as always, as with any adversity, there are people who will thrive. How? It's simple: they've learned how to do more in less time, and make more of an impact using less energy. Not because they are afraid of hard work or long hours, but because they know they have to release time, identify their real goals, and then work to achieve them. *CareerTracking* is written for those of you who want to count yourselves among this select group of achievers.

Question 2: Are There Really Any *Shortcuts* to Success?

Yes, there are. And if you're like most professionals today, you need shortcuts. Let's face it, there are scores of books on each *one* of the topics we present in *CareerTracking*. But considering the professional magazines you have to read, not to mention the avalanche of memos, reports, and proposals — when are you going to find the time to wade through all these books, much less read them?

Well, now you don't have to, because we've done it for you.

Professional development is our business. We're immersed in success information day in and day out — we research it, work with it, use it, and love it. We consider our company, Career-Track, a laboratory for testing and improving our ideas. In fact, this book grew naturally out of the mission of our company, thus the name, *CareerTracking*. The title seems particularly appropriate because of the action it suggests. In addition, it's a term that we feel describes an as-yet-unnamed process (moving up in your career), much like 'networking' did in the early eighties.

We designed *CareerTracking* to separate the wheat from the chaff, to present all the facts but none of the fluff. As a result, we believe this book is the most concise, hardest-hitting success education available anywhere.

Look at the table of contents and you'll see another reason we call these skills shortcuts. All of them are skills which, though necessary for professional success, are never taught in school and rarely taught on the job. The fact is, those who learn them generally do it through years of trial and error. Our book is designed to save you the trouble.

An Unusual Format

CareerTracking presents information, not just so you can learn it, but so you can use it. That raises an important point about business (and, we suspect, life in general): success is achieved by activists. One of the most fascinating discoveries we've made is that success is a lot easier than it's cracked up to be. It isn't the result of a high intellect or sophisticated ideas. In fact, the crucial difference between successful people and unsuccessful people is that successful people *use* what they know — relentlessly.

CareerTracking presents information simply and consistently to make using it as easy as possible. Each chapter is divided into two parts. Consider the first part the 'pay-off'; its purpose is to 'sell' you on the value of the Success Shortcut and point out the many applications it has in your life. That is followed by a series of specific action points, called the How-To-Do-Its, which lay out, step by step, how to incorporate the knowledge and make it your own. This is the meat of the message, the action triggers that will lead you to higher effectiveness in each area. It's straight advice you can digest quickly.

The section of the book entitled 'To Become an Expert' is an annotated list of books that you can use as an ongoing resource. As the founders of CareerTrack, our business is keeping up with the latest in self-help and professional development products. These are the best we've found. Whenever a topic interests you or you'd like to become a true expert, make the time to investigate our recommended selections.

Core Beliefs Reflected in *CareerTracking*

The following six points make up the basic philosophy behind the ideas presented in *CareerTracking:*

Core belief 1: Success is the process of overcoming obstacles, and all are surmountable. All are also natural. Take office politics, for instance. Power plays, back-stabbing, and covert activities permeate every organization — why should yours be any different? Conflict is an unavoidable by-product of human beings working together. You can't back down and still get ahead. Yet most people underestimate their power in a conflict and therefore settle for less. They often blame themselves for being 'wrong' and, as a result, lose their confidence just when they need it most. Dealing with obstacles, not resenting or avoiding them, is one quality that separates winners from losers.

Core belief 2: There are no victims. In a free society everyone has choices. Nobody is the victim of an unreasonable, obstructionist boss unless he or she chooses to be. No one is trapped in a dead-end job or stagnant career without his or her own permission. *CareerTracking* will encourage you to seize the control you already have in your life and invoke your right to the pursuit of happiness.

Core belief 3: Success is simple. Not easy, simple. To paraphrase a Tom Peters truism, success skills add up to 'a blinding flash of the obvious'. They include persistence, paying attention, calculated risk-taking, smart work (and, yes, some *hard* work), optimism and activism. *CareerTracking* will help you fight your tendency to overcomplicate success.

Core belief 4: It's not what you know, it's what you do with what you know that counts. If there's one thing we believe totally after training over a million people, it's that successful people are without exception initiators. They create and exploit their own opportunities. *CareerTracking* promotes the belief that life is too short, and too easy, to wait. To quote a three-word philosophy on a sign in the author's office: 'Do Something Now!'

Core belief 5: All business is people business. Somewhere along the line most people get the impression that business is numbers, percentages, and bottom lines. It's not; business is people — and people, unlike numbers, can be unpredictable; unfair, and ego-driven. They also can be decent, committed, and caring. To make it even more interesting, we usually encounter both sets of qualities in the same person. Success comes from bringing out the best in people.

Core belief 6: There's never been a better time to achieve success. The world is changing right before our eyes. And with change comes opportunity. These days, if you have persistence and natural common sense, you can create success in your life. In fact, if you practise half of what you learn in this book, you'll have more options for success than you could ever act on. *CareerTracking* is meant to be as inspirational as it is educational.

How to Use *CareerTracking*

It will take you less than five minutes to read each of the twenty-six Success Shortcuts. But reading is just the beginning. We suggest you reread each shortcut once, making notes as you go. Think about how you are going to integrate the information into your own career. What, specifically, are you going to do differently? To what degree? When?

That's a big order, and it's a good reason to resist reading the whole book before you've taken the opportunity to actually use the information in any one chapter.

Again, *CareerTracking* is to be *used*; don't just read it and put it on the bookshelf. Keep it handy and refer to it when you need help. Or lend it to a friend when you want to give help.

There is no question in our minds that the ideas in *CareerTracking* are the forces behind our own success. There's

also no question that they will result in success for anyone
else who practises them. And that means you.

Jimmy Calano   Jeff Salzman

Boulder, Colorado

Break Bad Habits and Build Self-Esteem

The Keys to Self-Improvement

High self-esteem is like money in the bank.
— MARILYN FERGUSON, *THE AQUARIAN CONSPIRACY*

Throughout *CareerTracking* we shall present specific strategies for self-improvement. It makes sense that we should begin with a look at the key factor that determines whether self-improvement can even take place in your life. That factor is your own self-esteem. Developing positive habits and skills — whether it is managing stress, overcoming procrastination, or learning dictation — depends on your self-esteem. The higher your self-esteem, the more easily you will be able to integrate and benefit from all the new skills we present in this book. Conversely, the more you integrate and benefit from these new skills, the higher your self-esteem. It's a circular, self-perpetuating process that can work wonders in your life.

For that reason, building your self-esteem is the most important 'shortcut to success' of all. It will change your entire approach to life. When your self-esteem is high, you face problems by solving them instead of placing blame. High self-esteem means putting yourself out there instead of hanging back and wondering. It means when you fail, you learn from it and try again and again and again until you succeed, instead of stopping or, worse, never trying in the first place.

With a healthy self-esteem, you'll find more meaning in your work; you'll be more on top of it. You'll face your day-to-day challenges with confidence, and bounce back after defeats. Also, the better you feel about yourself, the better other people will feel about you. You'll have more confidence to meet new people and deal more effectively with the negative people in your life.

The benefits of a high self-esteem are clear. But how is it developed? Well, the process has been going on for a long time. Based on the messages you have received all your life from your parents, teachers, friends, the mass media, and your environment in general, you have developed certain beliefs about yourself and how you fit into the world.

If you are like most people raised in this society, many of your beliefs about yourself are probably out-of-date. Others may be downright destructive. It's no secret that lots of otherwise competent people sabotage their chances for success and happiness with certain hang-ups. That's because for most of us, unfortunately, our low self-esteem has been with us so long it never occurs to us that we can have any influence over improving it. Consciously or not, we accept feeling bad as our cross to bear.

But the truth is, none of us is trapped anywhere we don't want to be. Accepting this fact alone seems to be what separates successful people from those left playing the role of victim. Now, certainly, changing bad habits — whether they are money habits, work habits, eating habits, whatever — can be tough. But the higher your self-esteem, the easier it will be to do. One of the most exciting realizations you will ever have is that *you can change*. It may even turn you into a self-improvement addict. And why not? It's a great addiction.

Here are some of the essential 'how-tos' of building self-esteem. Take time to practise and master these principles, and not only will the rest of this book be more valuable, but your life will be better in every way.

THE HOW-TO-DO-ITS

1. Talk yourself up

There's a voice inside your head that chatters constantly (it's the voice that is right now saying, 'What voice?'). That voice, your 'self-talk', is integral to your self-esteem. Too often it's negative. It says things like, 'I'm too fat', I can't do this', or 'I'm tired' – the effect of negative programming, often left over from childhood.

Think about it yourself. If you were like most children, you were probably losing your toys all the time. You could never find your socks. The people around you, of course, were happy to supply a name for your problem — you were 'forgetful'. Over the years, forgetfulness became something of a joke. People would say, 'Johnny would forget his head if it weren't screwed on'. Perhaps forgetfulness became your little quirk, a handy and harmless conversation piece. But now, many years later, the prophecy has fulfilled itself. You are truly forgetful. In fact, it has become a comfortable and protected part of your entity, a little friend you can run to and hide behind when the going gets rough.

But being forgetful does not belong in the circles to which you aspire. Suppose the next time your boss asks you to explain a missed deadline you knock yourself lightly on the head ('Wow, I could have had a V–8!') and say, 'Oh, isn't that just like me! I would forget my head if it weren't screwed on!' You'll see what we mean by unacceptable behaviour.

'Forgetful' is just an example of the many labels people hang on themselves. Think about it again. What are the labels you have hanging on you? A good way to identify them is to listen to the way you describe yourself to other people. You may say thinks like, 'I leave everything till the last minute because I work best under pressure', 'I spend money the minute I get my hands on it', 'I just can't speak in front of large groups', 'I'm always late for everything', 'I can't resist chocolate', 'I'm just not the brainy type'. And so on. Do you really want to go through life with limitations like these? Shake them off!

The good news is that you can reprogramme your inner voice to build your self-esteem and create success patterns. The technique is to make positive statements (known as 'affirmations') to yourself. One good, all-purpose affirmation is 'I'm happy, I'm healthy, I feel terrific!' Say it over and over in your mind, or aloud — even write it down. The key is to say it in the present tense and with conviction. Anytime you hear your inner voice starting to put you down, stop it and substitute a positive statement on the same issue.

For instance, instead of saying, 'I spend money the minute I get my hands on it', try telling yourself, 'I'm an excellent money manager'. Instead of saying, 'I just can't speak in front of large groups', substitute, 'I love speaking in front of large groups, and I'm quite effective'. Instead of saying, 'I can't resist chocolate', substitute, 'I eat only wholesome and nutritious foods'. Even though these affirmations may not be technically true at that instant, telling yourself they are is the first step towards making them so. Try it and you'll see what a powerful device self-talk is in creating positive change.

2. Visualize the 'new you'

It seems that people are incapable of making changes that contradict their self-image. That's why a critical step of all self-improvement is to imagine yourself as if the improvement has already happened. This is called visualization. It is essentially the same principle as affirmation, except that instead of using words you use pictures. Want to be thinner and healthier? Visualize yourself that way. Want a promotion? Visualize yourself in your new role. Spend time with your image, going over the details and enjoying the new you. When you create and reinforce that image constantly, it will be easier to adopt the behaviours that support it — in fact, it will be irresistible. (See 'To Become an Expert', page 257, for sources of more information on the how-tos of affirmations and visualizations.)

3. Start small in most (but not all) cases

The natural inclination when making changes in your life is to get excited about it and *go all out*. You want to lose weight, so you completely stop eating. You want to be more productive, so you regiment your life so strictly there's *no chance* to waste time. While it is healthy to get excited about new commitments, it is usually impossible to keep them when they're so rigorous. And the first time you fail, you lose your enthusiasm and revert to your old ways. It's generally best to make major, permanent changes one step at a time. That way it's not such a shock to your system, and each small victory reinforces your commitment to making the next step. The one exception to starting small is in breaking addictions, the very nature of which is all-or-nothing. In these cases it is widely believed that 'abrupt cessation' is the best way to go.

4. Find people you can learn from

Obviously there are thousands of people who have faced the same problems and challenges you face. You can learn a lot by using them as examples. Chances are it's someone you know. If so, you may be able to develop a mentor/protégé relationship with this person. A mentor is your own personal teacher, counsellor, and guide. Usually it is somebody who has 'been there', who recognizes your potential and is willing to make a commitment to helping you achieve it. Another category of people you can learn from is your role model. As Laurence Olivier is to an aspiring actor, a role model may be someone you have never met but who has characteristics you admire and emulate.

While a mentor relationship can be hard to find, hundreds of role models are available to you at any time. They don't even have to be alive. Who are your heroes? Which figures in history have most intrigued you? Find out more about them. Read their biographies. Make it your hobby to become an expert on these people.

Start with the people you admire most — they're the ones you already identify with, and, therefore, they have the most to teach you. But don't limit your role models to 'great' people. There are many wonderful stories of ordinary people who have found a way to rise to the extraordinary challenges of life. Mentors and role models are rich sources not only of inspiration but also of the 'here's-how-you-do-it' guidance you need in your life. Why go it alone when you can have an army of powerful people walking beside you?

5. Step into a new arena

Often our self-esteem suffers because we become myopic about life. When we focus too intensely or too long on one particular area of life — be it career, family, or something else — we lose perspective. Minor things become huge, and events take on an importance far out of proportion to their real significance.

Sounds familiar? If so, it's time to step into a new arena. The possibilities are vast. Sign up for an outward bound course or some other wilderness adventure. When you're standing on top of a 14000-foot peak that you've just spent twelve breathless hours climbing, it's hard to feel quite so upset about the misunderstanding you had with your boss. Or volunteer to work (don't donate money, *work*) with a local charity. A couple of hours a week in a nursing home or hospice are worth years of psychotherapy when it comes to putting your problems in perspective.

Another way to step outside yourself is to develop an appreciation of the arts. The expression is that art 'moves' us, and in a sense that's literally true. Art reframes our existence in a larger context. It elevates us out of our circumstances of the moment and lets us see ourselves in relation to the higher truths. The effect is cathartic, leaving us refreshed and at times transformed. From music, to literature, to the visual and performing arts, there is a world of master work available. Have a taste of all of it, find what you like, and pursue it. Eventually you may even become a creator as well as an appreciator.

6. You're going to hear this a lot: Set goals

We know, it sounds like something you've heard all your life. There's a reason for that. It represents classic, proven wisdom that only a few seem to really understand: *People who set clear, vivid, measurable goals get what they want.* Goal-setting is a critical part of building positive habits and, therefore, self-esteem. A simplified yet complete goal-setting system is outlined in Success Shortcut 21.

7. Accept the bad times in life

Life is often unfair. That's tough to accept, because we have been steeped in the notion that, as enlightened people living in an enlightened society, we are somehow protected from injustice. But we're not. Certainly we all have more control over our lives than we often think. Yet there is a level at which we have no control, and this means there is still a lot of senseless, random pain and injustice flying around. It makes sense that from time to time some of it is going to hit us. There's nothing we did to invite it, and there's nothing we can do to stop it.

Life in general — and professional life in particular — demands a certain amount of equanimity. Get in touch with that part of yourself that is independent of the day-to-day ups and downs. Don't waste time gnashing your teeth and shaking your fist at things you can't control. Forget about luck. Forget about what you think life ought to be, and accept it for the exciting and unpredictable affair it is.

The fact is, you can *use* your moments of low self-esteem. Depression, the blues, anxiety — all alert you that something is wrong in your life, so that you can correct or rechart your course. So next time you're in a state, ask yourself, 'What's the lesson?' Examine the circumstances to see why you're feeling bad. Have you been honest with others? Are you being true to yourself? Are you an unwilling captive to someone else's goals? What's really going on here? In one way, life is absolutely fair: with pain comes growth. And the growth not only makes the pain hurt less, it also makes it useful and meaningful.

8. Get therapy

Sometimes you may find yourself facing a particularly difficult life challenge like divorce, loss of a job, or major illness. Or you may be battling a destructive habit like smoking, alcoholism, drug abuse, or overeating. In these cases, outside help may be the answer. Individual therapy, as well as support groups, is often quite effective in dealing with the major problems of life. Therapy no longer has the stigma it once had — in fact, many people today use it not only as a way to solve a problem, but as a means of ongoing personal growth. One thing is certain: no matter what you're facing, you're not alone, and there is someone out there who can probably help you. There are many organizations which help you find what you need.

9. Dramatize your commitment

Many times a little drama is just what the doctor ordered to get you off your established path. Want to be more productive? Spend a full Saturday reorganizing and relabelling your files. Want to lose weight. Buy a new coat that will fit only the thinner you. In this way you serve notice to yourself, and perhaps others, that this time you are committed to making the change. Whenever your commitment slips, you can remember the drama and get a fresh shot of enthusiasm.

You have to be careful that you don't get too dramatic in the process, however. About two years ago, Jeff, the author was committed to bodybuilding. He was tired of being a 180-pound weakling and wanted a few muscles on his skeleton. So he bought an expensive weight-lifting machine and used it ... for a couple of months. For the last two years it has functioned as little more than something on which to hang his clothes while he's dressing. The fact is, Jeff hates lifting weights — something he could have discovered about himself with a £50 introductory membership to a health club. So unless you want a £2000 clothes hanger in your life, be careful that you don't get carried away.

10. Overcome cravings

Cravings are your old habits' way of reasserting themselves. When they hit they hit hard, and it's easy to come to the conclusion that 'I can't live with this feeling'. The point is you don't have to live with it. Cravings, particularly substance (nicotine, alcohol, caffeine, etc.) cravings usually last less than two minutes. They trick you into thinking they're here forever, which is, of course, unbearable.

So when a craving hits, don't try to ignore it; in fact, focus on it and ride it out with confidence. Expose it for the paper tiger it is, and you'll eliminate its power to control you. This principle is probably the single most important key to Jeff's giving up cigarettes a few years ago. Whenever the craving hit, he would get up, walk around, and push himself through it. Sure enough, in a couple of minutes the craving would pass. In its place was a feeling of power over his addiction and control over his life, which is far more satisfying — not to mention healthier — than a cigarette ever was.

11. Try it for twenty-one days

New behaviours take a while to adopt. It's been shown that when a new habit is practised for twenty-one days, it is far more likely to be integrated permanently. At first, a new habit feels foreign and requires conscious effort, but after twenty-one days it becomes more a part of you, a part of your self-image. If you're really committed to making a change, make yourself live with it for at least twenty-one days.

12. Associate with positive people

So many people assume the 'victim' role in life. Low self-esteem makes them passive, then bitter, and ultimately they seem to take more pleasure in suffering over their problems than in solving them. Be careful when you're around people like this, because their affliction is contagious. Make it your goal to surround yourself with positive people — people who are excited about life and its possibilities. They'll support you in your growth and allow you to support them in theirs. That's a big part of what life and friendship are all about.

It's often said that true success is overcoming the fear of becoming successful. Many successful people suffer from what we call 'fraud guilt'. Perhaps you will recognize it in yourself. You experience fraud guilt when you believe you do not deserve what you've managed to achieve. You may feel that your success is all the result of a fluke, or came about because you were particularly adept at fooling people. Consequently, you live with the fear that someone is going to find out the truth and expose you to the world. Worse yet, down in the secret recesses of your heart you suspect that the world already knows you're a fraud and everyone is keeping it under wraps out of some sort of unspoken conspiracy of good taste.

There are four typical symptoms of fraud guilt. Number one: You stay in the background, away from the action, hiding lest someone should spot you for what you really are. Number two: You shy away from conflict, fearful that you might anger people sufficiently to make them expose you for what you really are. Number three: You avoid making decisions because you fear you'll make the wrong ones and everyone will see you for what you really are. Number four: Since your fundamental incompetence can't help but sometimes show through, you're haunted by mistakes and problems. You spend most of your time putting out fires and plugging the holes in the dyke rather than making things happen.

There are two cures for fraud guilt. One involves twelve years with a psychiatrist. The other — in our opinion far easier and possibly even more effective — is to look around you and see what an idiot everyone else is. We're serious. There's no quicker confidence builder than the realization that you're not the only one who thinks he or she has something to hide. Everyone must deal with the ghosts of insecurity and self-doubt. Well, almost everyone. There are a few fascinating exceptions — you'll know them when you meet them.

Initiate and Make Things Happen

Them That Does, Gets

Everybody wants to go to heaven,
but nobody wants to die.
— ANONYMOUS

'He's a go-getter.' 'She's an accomplished woman.' 'They certainly know how to get things done.' We often hear these phrases. They reflect our society's fascination with and respect for achievement. But how does achievement happen, and what is it really that separates achievers from the multitudes stuck spinning their wheels?

Harold Geneen, the man who led ITT Corporation from $66 million to $22 billion in sales, puts it best: 'The purpose of a professional is to do what it takes to make things happen.' Not *whatever* it takes in the sense of unethical behaviour, but *what* it takes, in the sense of biting the bullet, rolling up your sleeves, digging in, and most of all taking initiative.

Unfortunately, many people are still standing around and waiting. Alvin Toffler, in his bestselling book *The Third Wave*, writes that one of the main reasons people have a hard time taking initiative is that our educational system doesn't reward initiative. In fact, he says, in many ways it *punishes* initiative. As Toffler points out, our approach to education was based on the needs of an earlier time, the Industrial Revolution. And the purpose was basically to teach two things: first, to do repetitive work by rote, and secondly, to be prompt about it.

Think about your own twelve- or sixteen-plus years of school. You were given an assignment and you were told exactly what to do (remember asking the teacher, 'Is this report supposed to be three pages or four? Typed or handwritten? Single-spaced or double-spaced?') You were told where to find the information, you did it, you handed it in, you got your mark, and you were done with it. Right?

In the real world, particularly when you are an initiator, it almost never happens that way. As the initiator, you are giving yourself assignments; you almost never know exactly what you have to do. Think about your own job situation. Imagine yourself behind your desk right now. There are probably a hundred things you *could* do to be more effective. Which one should you do?

In the real world you almost never have enough information to make a decision. It is one of the strange paradoxes of our time that we're living in the information age — we're drowning in information — and yet we still never have enough of it. In the real world, as an initiator, sometimes you have to make decisions and take action based on insufficient information. The only thing worse than a bad decision is no decision. (Have you ever heard of the 'paralysis of analysis'? It immobilizes a lot of people.)

In the real world you almost never know when a project you initiate is due, because you're setting your own deadlines. In some cases you never know when it's done, because something can always be done better — and in the real world you may not know how well you've done for weeks or months, or even years.

The real world is a strange, nebulous environment that immobilizes a lot of people. Raised and trained in a school system where they were told what to do, a lot of people find it impossible to take any independent action whatsoever.

Now, let's look at the other side of the coin, the initiator. Successful people — achievers — have one crucial characteristic in common: they are constantly looking for new ways to impact their environment. The initiator knows that there are dozens of opportunities to initiate in every organization. It's a way of looking at the world that spawns not only major breakthroughs, but a steady stream of small gains (which in retrospect often look like breakthroughs).

When you decide to initiate, you become a player instead of a spectator. And though taking initiative certainly has its material rewards, the good feelings of accomplishment and control over your life are even better.

It can even become habit-forming, as it has for Jimmy,

who says it all started for him with a high school sports pep talk, which he now refers to as 'The Do-Something Pep Talk' that changed his life.

The talk was delivered by Jimmy's track coach, Mr. Baron, who turned out to be Jimmy's first mentor. Mr. Baron had excelled in athletics in high school, gone off to college, and later returned to teach and coach at his old high school. He was a big-brother figure to most of his students, and often coached them in life as well as athletics.

Coach Baron's life-changing pep talk came during a team hurdle before the biggest meet of the season. It went something like this: 'So you guys all want to be Joe Hotshot in school, right? You want to read your name in the newspaper? You want to hold court with the prettiest girls? You want everyone to be impressed? Do you really want these things?' Every guy in the room would have committed murder for them! 'Then it's simple. *Just do something*. That's all it takes.'

His comments, of course, were in reference to the times, distances, and heights the team would strive for in the next day's meet. But beneath the surface, Jimmy realized, lay a profound principle of life. Coach Baron's words made it crystal clear to him that winners are separated from losers simply by what they achieve. His philosophy made sense. And in the next three years it certainly held true: when Jimmy scored well in a meet, all the glory and adulation flowed his way; when he did poorly, nothing happened and he remained unnoticed.

Jimmy carried his coach's 'do-something' philosophy with him beyond high school athletic competition.

In college, it inspired him to achieve high grades; in business, it's his central principle of success.

It can be yours, too.

THE HOW-TO-DO-ITS

1. Take on the undesirable

Some of the best opportunities for initiative lie in the projects nobody wants to handle. Volunteer! Since the job is seen as undesirable, people won't want to bother you. You'll be in a position to take charge and may turn the project into a major opportunity.

For instance, Linda, a friend of ours who had just started working in a retail store, volunteered to take inventory. The inventory job was frankly a big one, and being one of the most dreaded jobs in retail, naturally nobody wanted it. So they said, 'What the heck... give it to Linda'. She took it on and did a characteristically top-notch job. Soon she became the resident expert on inventory and inventory-control procedures. People came to her with questions and listened to her opinions. And, as often happens, building credibility in this one area gave her credibility in all areas. To cut a long story short, two years later Linda was running the store.

2. Look for trouble

One of the most powerful habits you can adopt as a professional is to stop yourself for one minute every hour and ask yourself, 'What's going on here?' Mentally step outside yourself and look at what you're doing; what your people are doing; even what your boss, competitors, suppliers, and customers are doing. What's not working? What could be made better? When you open your eyes — and, therefore, your mind — you'll see opportunities for initiative everywhere. The trick is to *do it*. You have to take your nose off the grindstone long enough to size up the situation. Force yourself at first, even if you have to get a digital watch and set it to buzz one minute every hour to remind yourself.

3. Don't wait to be trained

This is a crucial attitude for the initiator. Anytime you see a way, beyond your current duties, to make yourself more valuable to your organization, pursue it. Don't wait to be told (you may never be). Instead, ask questions and read everything you can get your hands on. Although your boss is responsible for training you, he or she most likely is not a professional teacher. Unlike your college professor, your boss may not be ready to give you a new assignment every time you're ready for one.

For instance, our creative director, T. Taylor, had been hounding us for six months to let him put one of our seminars on videotape. The problem was we didn't know how to help him get started. We didn't know anything about video production ourselves. Finally, he just grasped the opportunity. He wrote us a proposal, drew up a budget, and cornered us in the hallway one day and said, 'Here it is. I want to do it. Can I? Can I? Can I?' We had no choice. He had begun. So we said okay. And, three months later, he produced our first successful videotape — in about one-quarter the time and for one-tenth the budget that are typical in the video industry. As he proved, training and taking on new responsibilities are processes you must ultimately take charge of yourself.

4. Pay attention to the trade press

We know, we know — it's tough getting through the stacks of magazines and newspapers that land on your desk. But there's no better source of 'initiable' ideas. The purpose of the trade press is to report what's new in your industry. Who's trying what? What's working and what isn't? Trade magazines are *gold mines* of action stimulators for the initiator — often complete with the whys, wheres, and hows. Can you afford not to be informed? (For some good techniques on reading faster and more efficiently, see Success Shortcut 5.)

5. Be opinionated

Don't worry about coming across as pushy or overzealous. Speak with confidence. Assume your ideas will be listened to and respected, and you will have immediately increased your chances of its being true. This doesn't mean you have to have an opinion on everything (please, not that!), but if you have an insight and see an opportunity, speak up. If it turns out you were wrong, ask for clarification so you can learn from it. Offering your ideas is an initiative that can be very successful.

David, an acquaintance of Jeff's, is a good example of what can happen when you offer your opinion. A couple of years ago David was hired as a short-order cook at a restaurant in Rapid City, Michigan. A dead-end job right? Not for David. He's a bright person, and after serving up a few thousand sandwiches, knishes, and egg creams, he began seeing some weak spots in the system. Instead of ignoring the deficiencies ('It's not my job') or complaining self-righteously to his fellow workers ('Whoever designed this kitchen didn't know what he was doing'), he did the unexpected. He developed several specific, realistic recommendations for changing the food-service system, wrote them up — complete with diagrams and explanations — and took them, in person, to the president of the company that owned the restaurant.

David's actions would be viewed by some as impertinent (after all, who is a novice sandwich boy to tell the president of a restaurant chain how to improve his operations?), but the president didn't think so. In fact, he was so impressed he soon made David the kitchen manager. A year later, after many more freely offered and on-target opinions, David was made vice president in charge of operations for the restaurant chain, and is so valued that he has been put on a lucrative stock ownership plan to help ensure his loyalty.

To be successful as quickly as possible, you must do what David did: take charge of your career. Always look for ways to extend your authority and influence in your job. Consider your job description a definition of the base of your responsibilities, not the boundary.

6. Fail proudly

Every new action, every initiative involves a risk. As you know, things that look great in theory often don't work in practice. Consequently, you are going to be wrong a certain percentage of the time. But wrong isn't necessarily bad. In fact, you'll be in great company; superachievers generally have a long string of failures behind them. Learn to learn from your failures. As Donald and Elenore Laird wrote, 'If you are absolutely and thoroughly wrong, you have the good fortune of knocking against the facts that set you straight again'. Also, don't worry about your image.

7. Learn somebody else's job

What a way to demonstrate initiative! Make the time to learn a fellow worker's tasks and responsibilities, and your manager will love you (especially if you do it in your own time). This exposure will also give you a better view of the workings of the company by showing you new areas where initiative can pay off. How about learning some aspect of your boss's job and offering to take *it* over? That's the kind of behaviour that is richly rewarded in business.

8. Don't be perfect

There's something to be said for people who care enough to always do their best. And it's usually said with rises in salary, bonuses, perks, and accolades. If you're someone who strives for perfection, congratulations; you're already miles ahead of your peers. If you're someone who expects to achieve it, however, you're on the wrong track entirely.

There are two distinct approaches to excellence in the professional world: *practical perfectionism* and *neurotic perfectionism* (can you guess which one is better?). Neurotic perfectionists tend to feel they need to be the best at everything they do. In order to succeed, they have to somehow further the state of the art on every project. This unreasonable, idealistic expectation makes progress torturously slow. (You'll hear them say things like, 'It's not quite right yet. I'll have to come back and work on it some more later'.) Finishing something is almost impossible; after all, it's never quite perfect. As a result, the anxiety level of the neurotic perfectionist is high and productivity is low. In business, nine times out of ten an unfinished 'masterpiece' is worth a lot less than what a 'perfectly adequate' approach would have been.

Practical perfectionism, on the other hand, means commitment to excellence, attention to detail, and systematic, results-oriented work habits. It also means knowing when to quit. Often a project's final 10 per cent of quality requires as much energy as its first 90 per cent. You have to ask yourself if it's worth it. Sometimes it is and sometimes it isn't. A business letter, for instance, is generally meant to communicate information. A first draft most often suffices — just get your points on paper and send it off. When debating the benefits of a higher degree of quality in any endeavour, be sure you consider the energy required to achieve it. Look at it this way: When you get one thing done you've created the time to do another.

Allow us to hedge on one aspect of our argument. In the

first year or two of your career it is a good idea, if you must err, to err on the side of 'too perfect'. Considering the quality of work of most new college graduates, a 'perfect' job will definitely make people take notice. It is much better to learn your professional skills too well than not well enough.

9. Don't get hung up on breakthroughs

It's like perfectionism: debilitating. Jan Carlzon, the man who led the dramatic turnaround of the super-successful airline SAS, says success is a result of being 1 per cent better at 1000 things, not 100 per cent better at any one thing. Small initiatives are less risky, too, so it's easier to get support from other people and easier to redirect them if they go off course.

10. Give it a nudge or a tweak

Initiators never run the same lap the same way twice. They know that some of the best initiatives are small improvements to old projects. So think about the routine tasks you perform, reports you write, meetings you attend, etc. If you're like most professionals, you've stopped thinking critically about these routine tasks — you're just 'going through the motions'.

Don't let this become a habit. In fact, make it a habit to do exactly the opposite: take a few seconds to look with an initiator's eye at *everything* you do. See how it could be done better, in less time, or even if it ought to be done at all (few initiatives pay off better than eliminating work that no longer has to be done). A thirty-second fine-tuning that saves you an hour a year is the stuff on which empires are built.

11. Be Napoleonic

It's not only important that *you* take initiative; as a leader you also want to inspire your people to do so. One of the best systems we've found for doing this is a military principle called 'completed staff work', a concept supposedly developed by Napoleon. When you worked for Napoleon, you didn't go to him and say, 'Napoleon, we have a problem. The supply lines are cut off. Ten thousand men are starving. What are we going to do?' When you worked for Napoleon, you went to him and said, 'Napoleon, we have a problem. The supply lines are cut off. Ten thousand men are starving. Here's what I can do. We can do A, we can do B, or we can do C. I recommend option A.'

Completed staff work means, quite simply, requiring your people to come to you not only with a problem, but also with options and a recommendation. It's a key to getting your people to take initiative. Look at the advantages: first of all, it slows down those people who are more interested in the problem than the solution. Do you know people like that? They like problems; they like upsetting you with them — it's the most fun they've had all day! If they have to come to you with options and a recommendation, it's too much trouble. They'd just as soon solve the problem on their own.

Another benefit of completed staff work is that it gives you better solutions. Let's face it, your people are on the front lines of the problem. They'll often think of solutions that you may not have. And as a leader you want as many options as possible.

A third advantage of completed staff work is that it creates opportunities for training. Under normal circumstances we can train people for two weeks on a particular procedure, and if we're lucky, they'll remember some portion of it. But if we give them the benefit of that knowledge when they're in the thick of a problem, they'll remember it a lot better.

You can also use completed staff work when you go to *your* boss. When you present your boss not only with problems but also with options and a recommendation, one of two things will happen. One possibility is that you'll be right; and that's a feather in your cap. When you're regularly right on a particular issue, you might say, 'You know, I've been right on this kind of issue the last five out of five times. I feel I've got it down pat. Maybe I don't need to keep clearing with you.' That way you will have assumed a little more authority.

The second possibility is that your options and recommendation will be wrong, in which case you can create a teaching moment for yourself. You can say to your boss, 'OK, what wasn't I thinking of? What don't I know that you do know?' Your creating teaching moments may make your boss a whole lot more enthusiastic and effective as a teacher.

12. Pursue your passion

Otherwise, initiating is too much work. We're motivated by

things that matter to us. Identify the areas you feel passionate about in your life and career, and head relentlessly in that direction. Eventually you'll reach a position where you 'can't not do it', and that's when the ideas, the initiative, and the results flow. As we've already said, in the final analysis it is inspiration, not hard work, that makes things happen.

Get More Done in a Day

Make Each Day Count

One of these days is none of these days.
— OLD ENGLISH PROVERB

Whatever you do as a professional will involve managing resources. The most important of these resources is yourself. Managing yourself as a professional is an active exercise, something to be looked on coolly and objectively: 'OK, what I've got here in front of me is a certain amount of intelligence, energy, and skills. Now, how can I get the most out of them?'

The concept of managing yourself may seem to have a workaholic or neurotic edge. Actually, the opposite is true. Workaholics and neurotics are notoriously bad self-managers. The fact is that good self-management means working fewer hours, because you are getting more done in less time. It also means gaining a good understanding of your limitations and potential, and determining the role you want work to play in your life, thus freeing yourself from the anxiety of dealing with cross-purposes and unrealistic, self-imposed demands.

Ultimately, what you accomplish in your career is the result of what you accomplish in a typical day. That's where careers are made and fortunes are built. Engineering a good day in terms of sheer work output pays off in three ways.

1. You'll achieve more and enjoy it more. It's not only a matter of reaching your goals, but also a matter of happiness, fulfilment, self-respect, and yes, making a contribution to the world.

2. You'll make more money. Let's face it, you're paid according to your contribution. When you earn a reputation as a high-output professional, you can generally expect consistent rises and promotions. Getting more done in a day means you can have more 'worth-living-for' rewards and luxuries.

3. You'll be balanced. Increasing your daily productivity gives you more precious time to do the other things you enjoy, like spending time with your family, hobbies, community service, or just taking off (that's a wonderful use of free time, by the way). You'll achieve a balance which will lead to better health, a more positive attitude, and certainly less stress. Operating at peak performance will give you a sense of control over your life.

Self-management is an idea that will become increasingly important in the professional world as the pressure for efficiency grows, stakes are raised, and competition gets hotter.

THE HOW-TO-DO-ITS

1. Plan your day the day before

Make a list of your objectives, rank them according to priority, and write down the time you estimate each will take. And *don't kid yourself* (it's amazing how people consistently underestimate the time their tasks will take). Fill a day with calls and deadlines, and your major accomplishment will be a terrific case of frustration. Also, it's best to plan your day at the end of the previous day. This pays off in four important ways: You're more objective and less likely to postpone the high-payoff (but unpleasant) tasks. With a just-completed day fresh in your mind, you know where you are on projects, and priorities come naturally. You can leave the office mentally free, because all the ends are tied up. The next morning you will arrive and know exactly where to start.

Figure 3.1 illustrates the daily planning sheet which our company uses. It's simple (some planning systems take more time than they save) and, most important, it increases the likelihood that you and your people will get to and accomplish your high priorities. Feel free to recreate it, adapt it, or just photocopy it. But do use it, because it works.

2. Know your rhythms and moods

Think of yourself at six o'clock in the morning. How do you

function? When do you hit your stride, mid-afternoon or midnight? This is information you can use. Schedule routine tasks and appointments for your low-energy periods, and important tasks and meeting for when you're bright and at your best. Work *with* your daily rhythms and you'll be not only more productive but happier.

3. Deal with the worst first

Tackle the hairiest project first thing. Deal with unpleasant people and issues head on. Get your most dreaded assignments out of the way and your day will take off. You will have created a momentum that feeds off itself, and you'll complete the rest of your projects far more easily. When the worst is over, it's smooth sailing for the rest of the day.

4. Do a preview review

When you're commuting to work each morning imagine that you're actually commuting home. Run the day over in your mind: Everything went as planned, you met your deadlines, handled problems, and enjoyed yourself... and now you're basking in the feeling of having met the challenges of another day. A preview review makes even the most overcommitted day seem less intimidating, because you've actually created a mental programme that you will unconsciously follow. You'll be better prepared to make the most of your day no matter what happens.

5. Be ruthless with time-wasters

Considering the plethora of meetings, details, phone calls, and conversations most professionals face, it is entirely possible to have perfectly active days in which absolutely nothing is accomplished. Unfortunately, many succumb to this temptation. But don't let it happen to you. Get *ruthless*. Develop a mind-set that judges every activity in terms of whether it brings you closer, however minutely, to your goals. This mind-set enables you to see which meetings can be skipped, which appointments cancelled or cut short, and which projects streamlined. You'll know when to say no. Even better, other people will tune in to your no-nonsense approach and learn to respect your time as much as you do.

Date _____ _____ Day _____

DAILY PLANNING SHEET

Today's projects in order of priority:	Time allocated:
1. _____	
2. _____	
3. _____	
4. _____	
5. _____	
6. _____	

Today's phone calls:

1. _____	
2. _____	
3. _____	
4. _____	
5. _____	
6. _____	

Tomorrow's calls and projects:

1. _____	
2. _____	
3. _____	
4. _____	
5. _____	
6. _____	

Figure 3.1   Daily planning sheet

6. Become a dictator

You may not have access to a secretary or typing pool, but if you do, mastering dictation will enable you to double your daily output. A good dictator can turn out a one-page letter in a couple of minutes and knock out the first draft of a ten-page report in less than an hour. When you move from a written mode to a spoken mode you experience a dramatic increase in the quantity — and quality — of your communication. So overcome any dictaphobia you may have, put down your pencil, pick up your dictation machine, and start working. You'll find out more about the benefits of dictation in Success Shortcut 6.

7. Find out how you're spending your days

You may be surprised. The only way to know how you're really spending your days is to keep a time log. A time log need not be a permanent routine; it is merely a diagnostic tool. Here's how it works: for a full week write down, in fifteen-minute increments, everything you do in a workday. Most people resist time logs, thinking they take more time than they save. Not true! The cumulative time you spend may be only four or five minutes a day, yet it can help to save hours. A week's worth of time logs will reveal misplaced priorities, recurring time-wasters, and patterns of low productivity that you are totally unaware of. If you're like most professionals, you'll be horrified at what your time log reveals. But the truth will set you free — to engineer and orchestrate a day that lets you reach your potential.

In Figure 3.2 we've reprinted a sample time log that we use in CareerTrack's 'Getting Things Done' time-management seminar. Developed by Ed Bliss, it is particularly effective because it is a double-entry system: the first category deals with *what* you are doing, and the second deals with *why* you are doing it.

The log in Figure 3.2 is blank so you can photocopy it and find out how you're really spending *your* time. For just a week, begin each day with a fresh log and keep it handy. Bring it up to the minute every half-hour or so. If you can't remember what you did at a particular time, put down a question mark — don't put down what you *think* you were doing. Above all,

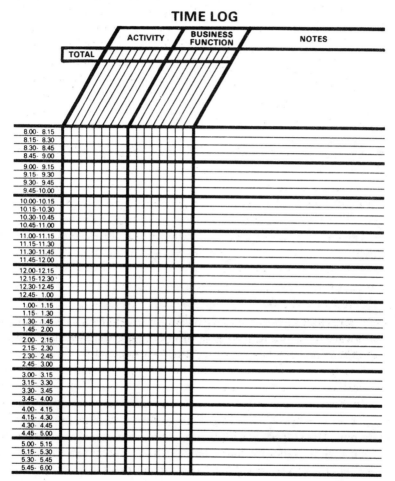

Figure 3.2   Time log © Ed Bliss

don't fill in the log at the end of the day, or you will be dealing
with fantasy, not reality.

At the end of the week, put all your time logs in front of
you and ask yourself the following questions:

- What am I doing that doesn't really have to be done?
- What am I doing that could be done by someone else?
- What am I doing that could be done more efficiently?
- What am I doing that wastes the time of others?

Don't put this exercise off. Start tomorrow. You'll find it's
quite an education!

8. Work with people who keep their word

That goes for fellow workers, employees, bosses, suppliers, and
even clients. When you know you can count on people to do
what they say they will do, you can in turn make commitments
and trust that things will, for the most part, happen as you
planned. One of our trainers, Susan Baile, said it best: 'If you
always do what you say you're going to do, I can build an
empire around you. If you sometimes do what you say you're
going to do, you're just another problem to me.'

Jeff learned, quite by accident, one of the best techniques
for getting people to keep their word. He was being called to
testify in a lawsuit brought against a former advertising client
of his. The client and Jeff had parted as friends, and Jeff wanted
to help him out as much as possible.

The lawyer for the opposition called Jeff, and in his most
authoritative voice said, 'Mr. Salzman, I need to have you in
my office tomorrow at 9.30 to give a deposition.' (A deposition
in the American legal system requires you to go to a lawyer's
office and, with both litigants and a court reporter present,
answer questions under oath concerning what you know about
a case.) Jeff knew enough about jurisprudence to understand
that he didn't have to present himself at 9.30 the next morning
— a deposition is given at the *witness's* convenience, not the
lawyer's.

Now you must understand that the American legal system
is a game. Jeff's role in the game was to be unavailable for
the deposition so his friend would have more time to prepare

his case. So he answered, 'I'm sorry, I can't make it tomorrow. I'm busy.'

'Okay, how about Thursday?' the lawyer responded, trying another gambit.

'Thursday? Busy all day.'

'Friday?' the lawyer asked.

'You should *see* my Friday — unbelievable!'

So the lawyer tried another tactic: 'Mr. Salzman, when can I see you in my office?'

Jeff responded, 'Two weeks from Thursday'. As they both were jotting that date on their calendars, Jeff was already thinking of ways to get out of the obligation so he could continue to be a 'good player'.

Just then the lawyer asked, 'Mr. Salzman, do I have your word?' Jeff realized he was playing with a master — and he had lost, because while a game is a game and the American legal system is as good a game as any, Jeff's word — his honour — was on the line. He was in the lawyer's office two weeks from Thursday, as promised.

Try this technique yourself sometime with one of your staff. Say you give somebody an assignment to be finished by five o'clock in the afternoon. 'Sure, no problem', they'll tell you. But when you ask, 'Do I have your word on it?' they'll often respond, 'How about first thing in the morning?' The point is, you were going to get it first thing in the morning anyway. When you ask people to give their word, you've increased immeasurably the chances of their keeping their promise.

9. Build in concentration blocks

To ensure that you get to your high priorities, *you must set aside a portion of your day to think, create and plan.* No interruptions, no phonecalls, no visitors, no distractions! Make an appointment with yourself, schedule a quiet hour, work at home, get to the office early or stay late. Most executives need at least two hours a day for this kind of focused work time. In fact, there will be days when you feel your only real accomplishment was made during your concentration time.

10. Play doctor

Most surgeons know two things about their day: firstly, they have to be in the operating room in the morning, and secondly, they have to be in their offices in the afternoon. You may be able to design your day in much the same way: concentration time in the morning, and meetings and appointments in the afternoon. This approach can free you from racing back and forth, both physically *and* mentally, from your desk to the conference room to outside meetings to the telephone — you know how it goes. An added benefit is that when you commit to blocks of time, your secretary or receptionist (if you have one) can schedule your appointments for you, freeing you from that time-consuming task.

For instance, Jeff's secretary knows that between three and four o'clock every afternoon, he's available for appointments. People in the company know that if they need to see him, they should ask his secretary to schedule some time. If people outside the company want to see him, they generally talk to his secretary first anyway. If she's not sure whether Jeff would like to have an appointment with a particular person, she will put a brief note in his basket saying, 'Would you like an appointment with this person?' and he'll reply either 'yes' or 'no'. She'll take care of the rest for him. All scheduling is done by her and all return calls, if an appointment has to be cancelled, are handled by her, which frees an enormous amount of time and energy for Jeff to do other things.

11. Organize your tools

By tools we mean whatever it takes to get the job done, anything from a wrench to a tax schedule. If you don't have them, get them. If you can't get them, then you should consider that maybe you are not equipped to do a particular job after all. Also, keep in mind that a desk is not a place to stack all the items you want to remember. It's a tool to expedite the receiving and processing of information. Have only one project on your desk at one time, and get rid of the things you're not ready to deal with right now.

12. Keep impeccable files

How easy it is to throw a report aside on your desk and say to yourself, 'I'll file it later'. 'Sure you will . . . maybe next month. You cannot be too compulsive about keeping your files up-to-date and accurate. This is the information age, after all, and a key aspect of your effectiveness is being able to put your finger on exactly the data you need. It takes a little more time in the short run to keep organized as you go, but doing so pays off in the long run.

We suggest creating a 'call-up' file to remind yourself of important deadlines and commitments. The benefit of using such a system is that you'll have a place to put documents you'll need in the future, along with a written reminder of what to do with them. You'll never be caught in the position of having forgotten to get back to a person or project. The call-up file is a classic tool for salespeople who want to stay in touch with — and keep important promises to — their customers.

Setting up a call-up file is easy. Create twelve files, one for each month, and label divider tabs, one for each date of the month. Then, place these divider tabs into the current month's file, and store the monthly files in chronological order in your desk. Whenever you know you'll need to call an associate or refer to/retrieve a document on a future date, jot down a note to yourself and place it into the file for that date. Then check your file every day to see what you need to do. On the first day of each month, move the dividers to the new month's folder, and file whatever notes or documents you have accumulated in that folder under the appropriate day. This simple system can remind you to do something up to a year from now. You'll never miss another deadline.

Beat Procrastination and Get Started

Getting It Done Now

To do nothing is in every man's power.
— SAMUEL JOHNSON

There's a simple reason most people never accomplish what they could — they just can't get started.

Almost everyone procrastinates from time to time, for many reasons. People procrastinate to escape unpleasant and seemingly overwhelming tasks, to get someone else to do them, or just because they are afraid of failing. Whatever the cause, the result of procrastination is always the same: frustration, anxiety — and too many missed deadlines.

The key to overcoming procrastrination is to *just get started*. Like most bad habits, procrastination is 'all in the mind', a problem more of perception than reality. After all, dreading work is always harder than doing it.

In fact, within a few minutes of working on a project, you generally get your second wind. Those of you who are runners, for instance, know that the first mile is always harder than the second. Getting past the barrier to your second wind is what overcoming procrastination is all about, because that's when you're warmed up, you've found your rhythm, and you're operating at peak efficiency. This is the state where working — like running — is a pleasure.

The result of overcoming procrastination, in addition to becoming more accomplished, is the satisfaction of knowing that you have entered — and can enter at will — a state of focused concentration and hyper-productivity. You've stopped all the elaborate excuses and avoidance games. You're no longer facing that awful night before it's due, and you're not missing the deadline. You're in control, and as a professional, that's where you belong. Don't let procrastination's bad habits and unrealistic fears keep you from achieving what you're easily capable of.

Again, the key is to get yourself started. Here are twelve insights and techniques that will help you start getting started.

THE HOW-TO-DO-ITS

1. Plot it out

The minute you take on a project, whether it's delegated or self-initiated, plot out the entire job on paper. That will make it more clear, tangible, and able to believe. Otherwise, when you get ready to start a task that has been unfocused in your mind, you invariably see that there's a lot more to it than you thought, and you procrastinate. Suppose you've decided to paint your living room. Seems simple enough, right? Start plotting it out. You'll see that the first step is choosing a colour, which means gathering up cushion and fabric samples to take to the paint shop. Step two is shopping; what exactly do you need in terms of brushes, etc.? Step three is moving and covering the furniture. As you can see, when you plot out a task you know *exactly* what's involved; you don't underestimate or overestimate it. Plus, you see easy ways to break it up (buying the paint tomorrow during your lunch hour, for instance).

2. Break it up

Anything is less intimidating when it is broken into pieces. If you have a big project hanging over your head, don't just say to yourself, 'I've got to get that project done'. Instead, tell yourself, 'This morning I'm going to outline part one on Table A'. That's a far more manageable task; and when you're done, you'll feel so much better about the project in general that finishing it, in this step-by-step manner, will be easier than you ever thought possible.

3. Do something now

For instance, if you decide to paint, gather your fabric samples right away, certainly before the day is over. Now the momentum is with you. Have to write a long report? Get all your resource materials together in one pile. Feels good, doesn't it? You've already started. The problem is it feels so good you may get smug about the project and think it's 'all under control', which is a terrific excuse for further procrastination. The solution: Start step two.

Have you ever heard of the American Famous Amos cookies? Created by Wally 'Famous' Amos, the enterprise was the first big success story in the gourmet cookie business. Do you know how he got started? He made a batch of cookies and asked his friends if they liked them. Then he telephoned potential supporters and suppliers, and one thing led to another. Now he's known worldwide for gourmet chocolate-chip cookies. Based on this experience he coined 'Amos's Law', which states, 'The best time to get started is when you have the idea'.

Just get started — dive in. If you lack all the information you'll ultimately need, you'll find out soon enough where to get it. Just begin somewhere, anywhere. And do it as soon as you get the idea. Otherwise, you're likely to procrastinate.

4. Make sure you can do the job

Before you take on a project, make sure you have the tools, expertise, and time required. For instance, Jeff had been putting off fixing a broken drawer for months when he finally admitted that he had neither the tools nor the expertise — nor the stomach, for that matter — to do the job. He decided that calling a carpenter was a more achievable task. The drawer was fixed the next day. Underestimating the time or effort a task requires, or overestimating your expertise and motivation, is the surest way to miss a deadline. Be realistic.

5. Remind yourself how good you are

Have to reprimand one of your staff? Remember, the reason you have to do this is because you've achieved management status. And one of the key reasons you've done this is because you're good with people — it's because you know, for instance, how to criticize people in a positive way. You have earned your position because you're good at it. Remember this, because when you're facing the tough parts of your job — the things you are most tempted to postpone — you need all the confidence you can get.

6. Do the distasteful first

If you're a chronic procrastinator, it's best to start your day with your most unpleasant job. Have to make peace with an angry customer? Pick up the phone the second you sit down at your desk. It's a tangible demonstration to yourself that, yes, you are capable of tackling the most distasteful tasks, and it makes the remainder of your projects seem that much easier. The ultimate goal is to change your way of thinking, from 'This is unpleasant; I don't want to do it', to 'This is unpleasant; I'd better do it now and get it over with'. Doing so frees you and creates the energy to do something else.

7. See it all done

It's been said that 'people procrastinate when they cannot anticipate achievement'. The following exercise helps you break through that barrier by showing you, in vivid detail, what achievement feels like. Close your eyes and relax ... Imagine that you have just finished your project, done a terrific job, and are basking in the good feeling of having achieved another goal. In your vision, focus on every process you went through to complete the task: the details, the hang-ups, the breakthroughs. Concentrate particularly on the elation of realizing your rewards. This simple visualization exercise makes any task seem less intimidating. Where you once felt only dread, you may begin to feel a flicker of enthusiasm.

8. Do it for ten minutes

The point is to simply make some progress, however small, on that project you've been avoiding. After ten good, solid, whole-hearted minutes (come on, you can do *anything* for ten minutes), reconsider. If you want to quit, go ahead and quit. Chances are, however, you'll realize that the job isn't so dreadful after all, and you will have gained enough momentum to continue.

9. Shout it from the rooftops

Committing yourself publicly is a negative motivator, in that your goal is not to gain a reward but to avoid a punishment: in this case, embarrassment. But it works. For example, if you've been putting off calling on three particularly difficult sales accounts, announce to your boss and fellow salespeople that you are going to make those your first calls today, and invite them to monitor your progress every week. Their support will spur you on. (This technique can be particularly powerful if the people you recruit happen to enjoy your failures.)

10. Reward yourself, or, if you prefer, bribe yourself

The next time you have an unpleasant task to perform, promise yourself a reward for getting it done by a certain deadline. This helps bring your goals into focus. The reward could be dinner out, a day off, or new clothes — anything that will motivate you. Upon completing your task you will be able to reward yourself freely and without guilt. Whatever you do, don't cheat by giving yourself the reward before you've finished (even though you're into bribery, you must maintain some pride). That would only reinforce your procrastination.

11. Become an automaton

This is a nasty, dehumanizing technique that may just work like a charm when all else has failed. Automatons don't worry about losing face with others, they have no concept of self-confidence, and they don't respond to rewards. All they know is 'do it'. That's how our friend Leonard describes this morning running routine: 'When the alarm rings at 5.30, I don't think about how warm it is in my bed and how cold it is outside. I don't think about maintaining my health or living longer. I allow no issues even to be raised for discussion. I simply reach out and turn off the alarm, get up and put one foot in front of the other.'

12. Find and finish what you've already started

What major project have you begun that you aren't aware of? Sometimes you may find that you've indirectly initiated something even as you thought you were procrastinating.

About a year after we wrote out first book, *Real World 101*, we talked about how we were going to write a second book. We talked and we talked and we talked, but we didn't do any writing. Book two just wasn't happening. We couldn't get started.

At the same time, we decided that we wanted to give our seminar attendees something extra, something they were not expecting. So we wrote a little pamphlet called 'How to Get Your Next Raise and/or Promotion'. We figured that topic would interest most people. We printed up a bunch of pamphlets to hand out at our seminars, and everybody loved them.

A few months later, we were really keen on goal-setting and were trying to get our employees committed to establishing objectives for themselves. That's when we decided to write another pamphlet, titled 'How to Set and Achieve Your Goals'. Then, a couple of months later, we decided to impress upon our supervisors and managers the importance of clear writing. So we wrote another pamphlet, called 'Write Easily and Be Understood'. A few weeks later Jimmy read a fascinating story on networking and decided to write a fourth pamphlet, on that topic. Halfway through the first draft, he realized we had begun our second book. We'd started but just didn't know it. Six months later, we had finished all twenty-six chapters.

Think about the projects for which you may already have dormant momentum. Could the memos you've been writing your staff be turned into a policy manual? Could the market research you've done on one area of your business be applied to another? How about previously abandoned goals? Consider the once critically important project you undertook but stalled on because you didn't have enough information or the right tools at the time to complete it. Never let work go to waste. Resurrect it. Find a new application. Leveraging work you've already done is one of the two or three most powerful success principles available to you.

Read More in Less Time

Master the Information Age

*You are the same today that you'll be five years
from now except for two things: the people you meet
and the books you read.*
— MAC McMILLAN

The information age is here. You've seen it yourself. In the scores of professional magazines you should be reading. In that stack of mail on your desk that seems to get taller every day. In the books you've bought but haven't found time to read.

Surviving and thriving as a professional today demands two new approaches to the written word. First, it requires a new approach to *orchestrating* information, by skilfully choosing what to read and what to ignore. Second, it requires a new approach to *integrating* information, by reading faster and with greater comprehension.

Like most professionals, you probably spend a solid 30 per cent of your working time reading (reports, letters, articles, whatever). That's why reading faster can be such an advantage. Tripling your reading speed — a fairly typical result of using the skills outlined in this chapter — will save you one full work day a week. You'll have an extra day to spend, not taking in information, but *using* it (remember, it's not what you know that counts, but what you do with what you know).

The brain is capable of processing well over a thousand words per minute, yet the average reading speed is only about 250 words per minute. The problem is that slow reading leaves your brain open to distractions. Therefore, when you move your reading speed from first to third gear a synergy of benefits accrues. You'll increase not only the sheer volume of your reading, but also your comprehension, retention, and enjoyment.

Advanced reading skills will pay off in all areas of your

life, because reading exposes you to mankind's greatest ideas. Reading is not only a source of professional information but a source of wisdom, your way of visiting other lands and ages, and enjoying history's 'greatest hits' of entertainment. If you value reading, you'll appreciate being able to read more in less time.

THE HOW-TO-DO-ITS

1. Set up a reading centre

This is a place in your home or office which is furnished and set aside for the sole purpose of reading. A good reading centre has four essential components: 1 *Quiet*. You must be able to relax in your reading centre and count on a block of uninterrupted time. That way, simply being there will signal your mind to put itself in a less distracted, more concentrative mode. 2 *Comfort*. Not only a comfortable chair, but also adjustable, nonglare lighting. 3 *A dictionary*. Don't pass over words you don't understand; each new word is an opportunity to improve your vocabulary and participate more fully in the richness of language. 4 *A means of recording information*. A pen and paper, dictation machine, whatever is convenient for you to record your reactions to what you are reading.

2. Clock your speed

To measure your progress, you must know what your current normal rate of reading is. Here's a simple way to calculate it: Read a non-fiction book for exactly one minute and stop (don't read faster than usual or you'll defeat the purpose). Then count the number of words you've read, and record it on a sheet labelled 'Reading progress'. Test yourself each day for six weeks and fill in the results. Keeping scores like this will give you instant feedback on how fast you're progressing, and will keep you committed to your speed-reading goals.

3. Watch your eye movements

Reading occurs when your eyes stop, ever so quickly, and focus on a word or group of words. Slow readers may stop ten or more times per line, while the speed-reader stops only two or three times. The trick, obviously, is to increase the number of words you take in at each stop *and* to move your eyes faster from stop to stop (including from the end of one line to the beginning of the next). This will seem easier after you have mastered point four.

4. Become comfortable 'missing' words

In infant school we were taught to read each word. That's appropriate for *learning* to read. However, for taking the next step in reading — speed-reading — exactly the opposite is true. reading takes place in your brain, not your eyes, so enormous speed can be gained by reading 'thoughts' rather than words. By allowing your brain to identify and absorb complete ideas you'll automatically quicken your eye movements, thus increasing your reading speed. Trust that your brain will know which words to pay attention to. It will.

5. Don't vocalize — even silently

One reason many readers have trouble breaking their habit of reading every word is that they 'say' each word in their mind. Again, what worked in learning to read ('sounding it out') holds us back in improving the process. Research has shown that your mind does not have to 'hear' a word to understand it. Demonstrate this to yourself right now by glancing at a word on this page and instantly looking away. Do it a few times until you understand how it is to 'see' a word without 'hearing' it.

6. Stop regressing

Regression means going back and rereading what you just read. Like vocalization and short eye movements, this is usually a result of a compulsion to 'get' every word on the page. The best way to break the regression habit is to force yourself to keep going. Practise this. At first you'll have the feeling you're missing something important. But soon you will develop the habit of forging ahead unless you have reason to regress.

7. Use your finger

Again, forget about what your infant teacher said. Running your index finger steadily and lightly under the lines of text, using it as a pointer, is one of the keys to faster reading. It minimizes regression, provides a visual anchor to keep your eyes from wandering, and lets you push your eyes steadily beyond your normal reading speed. It also helps you increase your concentration by adding another sense — touch — to the act of reading. Here are two helpful hints for using your finger in reading: First, move your hand from the elbow, not the wrist; and second, lift your finger when returning it (quickly!) to the left margin. It may feel awkward at first, but after a few pages you'll get the hang of it.

8. Preview, review, and record

To get the most out of your reading, you must get involved with it. Before you start, preview the cover copy, introduction, subheads captions, bold type, and summary paragraphs. Then immerse yourself in the reading material, underlining passages you feel are important. After each section, sit back for a few minutes to identify your thoughts or feelings, sum up the author's message, and criticize the work. Record your insights and keep them; you'll be surprised how often you refer to them. Reading this way may take a little longer, but you will substantially increase your comprehension and retention.

9. Practise, practise, practise

Speed-reading is a skill which can be learned and improved. But the only way to do so is to read regularly, practise the techniques explained above, and push your speed. To increase your current speed by two to three times, you'll need to spend about thirty minutes per day for six weeks. That's fairly small time investment for a pretty dramatic return.

10. Set your own speed limit

Not everything can — or should — be speed-read. Technical books, subtle passages of a novel, and fact-laden business writing often require careful, word-by-word scrutiny, with several regressions, to grasp the meaning. And who would suggest that poetry should be speed-read? You decide which speed is best, depending on the material. Soon you'll have the ability either to 'cruise' or take a 'Sunday afternoon drive' through the words.

11. Don't even read it

If you'd like to take speed-reading a step further, here's a way to knock out 50000 words a minute. All you have to do is recognize, within one minute, that a particular 50000-word book does not suit your purposes, and decide *not* to read it. To thrive in the information age, you have to know how to choose what to read. Become ruthless. One good book on a subject will probably tell you all you need to know. And don't fall into the trap of feeling you have to read every paragraph or finish every book you start. Often skimming can give you 80 per cent of all the important information a book or article has to offer, at a fraction of the time. This is speed-reading at its best. (Use the time you save to decide how to *apply* what you're read.)

Jimmy subscribes to over 25 business magazines, trade journals, and newsletters to stay on top of his job. Unfortunately, he also has to manage the company and cannot spend four hours a day reading everything that's published on professional development and direct marketing. After seeing his reading stack grow taller and taller and discovering articles of critical interest *months* after they had been published, he thought, 'There has to be a way to keep up with all this reading!' There was.

He decided to have his secretary photocopy the table of contents of every publication that he receives. Now when he's reviewing his mail, he skims through the various tables of contents looking for articles that interest him. Knowing how limited his reading time will be, he circles only articles which directly affect his work — the ones he *needs* to read. His secretary will then photocopy the articles he requests. This spares him from having to cart around large numbers of periodicals in his briefcase, flipping through thousands of pages of advertisements, and falling prey to the temptation of reading articles of only minor interest at the expense of major ones. Now he has to contend only with a thin file of current articles on subjects of high interest. In a sense, he and his secretary create their own personalized magazine each week.

There's a side benefit to using this reading system. When you finish each article, you either can toss it, route it, or make more copies without having to locate the original publication. It really works.

12. Don't let up

Once you've mastered effective speed-reading skills, it's still easy to slip back into old, bad habits. Discipline yourself to keep your speed-reading skills sharp and ever-improving. Test and record your speed from time to time. If you catch yourself reading without your finger, or reading an article without skimming it first, correct yourself. Like all good habits, speed-reading requires constant reinforcement.

Dictate and Double Your Productivity

The High Achiever's Secret Weapon

*Those who shy away from dictating go through life
driving oxcarts instead of jets.*
— JEFFERSON D. BATES, *DICTATING EFFECTIVELY*

The above quote sums up the power of dictation. The fact is, with dictation skills you can double your productivity. Hard to believe? Look at it this way: Imagine that for the rest of the day everything you communicate has to be written. Instead of picking up the telephone, you must write a letter. Instead of talking to someone, you must write a memo. You're going to get a lot less done, aren't you?

That's precisely why dictation is so advantageous. It moves you from a written to a spoken mode. The result? A dramatic increase in both the quantity and quality of your communication. Can you afford not to have this kind of advantage? Consider:

- How long does it take you to write a one-page letter? A good dictator can do it in a couple of minutes.

- Feeling guilty about those projects that just aren't getting done? With dictation you can knock out the first draft of an eight- or ten-page report in about an hour. Spend another half-hour editing, and it's done. Specific projects vary, of course, but one thing's certain: The bigger the project, the more dictation helps.

- Tired of letting good ideas get away or go undeveloped? Most people don't think of dictation as a tool for creativity, but it's one of the best. Don't let aching fingers slow your racing mind. Dictation lets you relax so your natural creativity comes through.

- Want to stop wasting time in traffic, at airports, etc.? Turn wasted time into productive time, with your dictation machine.

- Need facts at your fingertips? Dictate notes after

phone calls, meetings, negotiations — and you'll always be the one in control of the facts.

No wonder we call it the high achiever's secret weapon. The fact is, dictation has long been the productivity/ creativity tool of doctors, lawyers, and top executives — all professionals known for high output, high prestige, and high salaries. Look around and you'll find an obvious correlation between those who dictate and those who succeed.

Here's a good example: Jimmy has a slight vision problem, and every three or four years he seeks out a specialist to learn if a breakthrough operation has been discovered. A few years ago, he went to his family eye doctor and asked, 'Who's tops in Denver?' The doctor gave him a specialist's name but added, 'He's £70 for a fifteen-minute appointment', which was about three times the rate a family doctor would charge. Jimmy made an appointment anyway; after all, it was his vision they were talking about.

When he arrived at the office, he was mightily impressed. It was outfitted with the most elaborate equipment he'd ever seen (and he considers himself an expert on eye doctors' offices, because ever since he was little he has been paraded through a lot of them in his search for a cure). The doctor gave him the most thorough examination he'd ever had, *dictating notes all the while*, using a strategically positioned foot pedal to activate the microphone. The doctor even dictated a letter to Jimmy's family doctor telling him what he had found.

It turned out there was no new miracle operation, but Jimmy felt reassured by the completeness of the examination. He was also impressed with the doctor's efficiency and now knows why he is considered the best in the state. He made every second count and was *worth* the $70.

Look at the advantages the doctor gained by dictating on the spot: 1   His notes, and even letter, were done when the examination was over. The doctor didn't have to worry about any paperwork or homework on Jimmy's case. All he had to do was sign the letter after his secretary typed it. 2   He was sure not to forget or mistake any facts, because he dictated what he found *immediately*. He did not have to piece together facts hours later. 3   He could concentrate better, because he didn't have to stop and make notes during the exam. He could 'flow' more easily in a creative, observant mode. 4   In this case (which doesn't necessarily apply to business) he was communicating with his patient as he was dictating. This effectively stripped away a lot of the mystery Jimmy felt with other doctors, and made him an insider in his own treatment. Also, at the end of the exam, the doctor was free to give Jimmy his full, undivided attention (no notes, remember?) and answer his questions.

Most of these advantages, and a few more, are easily available to you in your profession. Invest the time to learn the art of dictation and you'll wonder how you ever did without it.

THE HOW-TO-DO-ITS

1. Get the Mercedes of machines

Buy the best you can afford (the first time your cheap machine breaks when you're in the middle of a project, or eats a finished tape, you'll wish you had). There are two basic types of dictation machines: the desk-top model and the portable, hand-held model. If you can afford only one, get the portable. It's important to be able to carry your machine with you — you never know when inspiration will strike. Features and quality vary enormously, so investigate before you buy. The fancier machines can, among other things, warn you before the end of a side, mark the beginning of each message for easy retrieval, and let you dictate different messages to four different people without changing tapes. These features are all worth investing in. You will also have to choose between mini- and micro-cassettes. We recommend micros, because both the cassettes and machines are more compact.

2. Deal with 'dictaphobia'

Many professionals have a fear of dictation. When the microphone goes on, their mind freezes. Even if you consider yourself a hopeless dictaphobe, you'll find yourself dictating like a veteran if you do the following: 1 *Start by reading* into your machine — a magazine article, old memo, anything just to get started. 2 *Get a mental picture* of your audience — pretend it's a conversation and you'll speak more easily and naturally. 3 *Don't worry about getting it perfect* — you can always edit later. Dictate just as you talk; use simple English, even clichés and sentence fragments — whatever you need just to keep moving. 4 *Be patient* — dictating feels odd at first. So did riding a bicycle; but once you got used to it, it certainly beat walking.

3. Get organized and prioritized

To keep yourself on track while dictating, it helps to have a written outline of what you want to say. For short memos and letters, a simple laundry list of 'cues' will do. For reports and speeches, you'll need a more detailed outline (try index cards — you can lay them out on your desk in just the right order and dictate from there). If you think you'll need reference materials or files, have them handy. Putting all your references and notes at your fingertips will save you from having to fill in the blanks later on.

4. Use this system

To make dictation really work, you need a system for keeping track of your tapes and documents. if you have an important document and forget which tape it's on, you're in trouble. Follow these four simple steps and you'll always be on top of your dictation: 1 Code each message and corresponding document, beginning with, for instance, 01/3–10 ('01' indicates the first item; '3–10' is the date). Make a written list of this information and give it to your transcriber. 2 Add to your list the number on the machine's counter at the start and end of each document (e.g. from 000 to 024 is a letter to Bob, from 025 to 061 is a memo to Sue, etc.). This will help your transcriber quickly locate your priority items. 3 Mark each cassette with a small Post-It note containing the date and any further identification. 4 Don't erase the tape until your dictation is typed and out the door — you never know when you'll misplace a draft and wish you had the original tape. With this system, you'll never forget a detail, never be at a loss for a fact, and have all the information on even the most complicated deals at your fingertips.

5. Give nothing-left-out instructions

Whether you're talking computers or dictation, the rule of thumb is 'garbage in, and garbage out'. With that in mind, start your dictation by identifying yourself and giving general instructions: first, the type of dictation (whether it's a memo, letter, report, etc.); next, approximate length, format in which you want it printed, return addresses, heading, draft number, number of copies, routing list, enclosures, and anything else you can think of that will prevent your transcriber from having to guess. Be sure to dictate any special punctuation, too. Never assume your transcriber will punctuate your writing the way you envisage it. Also, remember to *enunciate* and s-p-e-l-l anything that could possibly be misunderstood.

6. Watch your pace and pauses

In consideration of your beloved transcriber, speak at a normal rate — about 125 words per minute. This way he or she can go with the flow, and won't have to backpedal because you're talking too fast. Be sure to press the pause button (or on/off switch) when you stop to think — unless you want your transcriber to strangle you with the tape. Nothing is more frustrating than listening to dead air while waiting for a recorded message.

7. Don't be a windbag

When dictating you may tend to say a lot more than you would in writing. After all, it's easy to sit back and ramble. Remember, though, somebody's got to type it *and* somebody's got to read it. Save your transcriber cauliflower ear and your reader eye strain. Get into the same 'just-the-facts' mentality you would use when actually writing a letter, memo, or report.

8. Edit like crazy — later

Plan at least two drafts for everything you dictate — especially if you're new at it. What makes dictation really work is the interaction between the creative (speaking) mode and the critical (editing) mode. Never try to edit as you dictate — it's extremely difficult to edit something you can't see. Dictation, like writing, is a two-step process. First, get your ideas down, and then polish them. Also, ask your transcriber to double- or triple-space the first draft, as it makes editing — and retyping the edited copy — much easier.

9. Use dictation to delegate

Leaving town? Forget about writing a long memo of instructions the night before you leave. Dictate it. Getting ready to delegate an important project? Dictate the instructions and your staff can replay them whenever they need to (without interrupting you with questions). In fact, try labelling separate tapes with the names of every person you work with. Whenever you wish to communicate a message to one of them, just pop in the appropriate tape and start talking. And why not encourage them to send tapes to you? You can now all communicate with each other when it's most convenient.

10. Don't dread it, dictate it

Dictation is a fabulous cure for procrastination. Start by making a list of all the projects you've been putting off, and then pick up your machine. Start dictating the steps you'll take to achieve each goal. You'll be surprised at how precisely you know what needs to be done. Have it transcribed and then take action. How? By dictating *what* you need to do, *how, with whom, by when.* Simply dictating your plan will move you one step closer to completion. And because dictation saves time, you'll have more time to get down to what you've been putting off.

11. Have a dictation brainstorm

Don't let a good idea get away. Dictation enables you to capitalize on all your good ideas by 'getting them down on paper' without the paper! Get rid of distractions, lean back, put your feet up, grab your machine, close your eyes, and let loose. You'll be amazed at how ideas come pouring out of you when you let them flow at their natural speed, instead of slowing them down to match your writing speed. Dictating will unleash creative powers you never knew you had.

12. Dictate to yourself

If you don't have a secretary, you can still use dictation to increase your productivity. How? Send your dictation to a word-processing service, or, cheaper still, type it yourself. Either way you can still take advantage of the creative edge dictation gives you. You can use dictation to put commuting time to work. You'll also become more careful at dictation if you have to transcribe your own, which will pay off when you do get a transcriber. Plus, when you transcribe your own, you can edit as you type. It's much faster and easier than typing a first draft cold.

We'd like to leave you one final note on dictation: use it or lose it. As we said, dictation will feel odd at first. But persevere. In fact, make it a habit. By dictating every day at the same time, you will make it part of your daily work routine. Resist writing whenever you can in favour of dictation, your new secret weapon.

Manage Your Stress to Feel and Work Better

Achieve More, Enjoy it, Live Longer

Be cool.
— FATS DOMINO

Like most people you probably take pride in working at full throttle. If so, don't worry: This Success Shortcut is not meant to slow you down. In fact, it will actually help you move ahead faster.

Stress-management skills help you achieve more by showing you how to keep your energy level high throughout the day, improve your concentration and creativity, make better decisions under pressure, maintain your composure (even when others are losing theirs), make fewer mistakes, and relax and renew yourself quickly *on the job*.

In other words, stress-management skills get you more in shape for the top. Look at those who are already at the highest levels of your profession. Chances are they have a steadiness that other people respect and rely on. Unfortunately, many people stall on the organizational ladder because the can't 'keep cool under pressure'. What you learn in this chapter can help you develop the grace, energy, and style of today's super-achievers.

Stress management means you'll not only achieve more, you'll enjoy it more. People who know how to control their stress have more enthusiasm, energy, and vitality. Work is fun and exciting, something to look forward to. And their relationships on the job are more positive and productive, whether they're collaborating or competing. Stress management may not eliminate 'down' moments, but it will minimize them and make you happier.

One of the best benefits of stress management is that you'll live longer, or as Bob Hope put it, die young at an older age. Stress is known to contribute to most diseases. Don't make your body pay the price of your ambition. People who learn stress management can have more vitality in their forties than they had in their twenties.

Once you use the following principles and techniques in the office, you'll be surprised at the changes that take place. You'll notice you have a new energy, vigour, and purpose. You'll sense a difference in the way people react to you. You'll adapt better to change, and experience the excitement of being more *in control* of your work and your life.

Are results like these important to you? Keep reading.

THE HOW-TO-DO-ITS

1. Eat right: light

There are volumes of materials written on nutrition, and if you're like most people, you already *know* what's good for you. The trick is to *eat* what's good for you. Here are three simple nutritional tips that will help you get through the work day more smoothly, energetically, and productively: 1 Pick one item from each of the following categories for breakfast: fresh fruit; whole-grain bread, muffin, or cereal; low-fat yogurt, cottage cheese, or milk (soy milk is fine). The combination will provide a high, sustained energy level. 2 Eat a light, low-fat lunch — fish is great. Big meals, especially washed down with alcohol, contribute to sluggishness and afternoon fatigue. 3 Keep fresh or dried fruit in your office for a snack. It will get you through hunger pangs and even an occasional skipped lunch (in fact, two snacks are better than one big meal).

2. Break the vices

You've heard it before but we'll say it again. Alcohol fogs your mind. Tobacco saps your endurance and contributes to an early, gruesome death. Refined sugar lifts you up and slams you down on the mat. So does caffeine. Taking the two of them together (coffee and cakes) is like facing a Japanese sumo wrestler — do you really need that first thing in the morning? If you can't break these addictions totally, at least declare your office a vice-free zone. Consider your workplace a healthful environment, and you'll not only do better work, you'll be able to expand from there to a more positive lifestyle overall.

3. Make sure you fit

There are all kinds of people and all kinds of organizations. It's critical to find the right fit. A Type A person (driven, fast-moving) in a Type B environment (laid-back, slower) will be stressed — and will cause stress. The same is true of a Type B person in a Type A environment. Look around your office. Do you like the pace of work? Do you like the people? Do you agree with their values? If not, consider changing jobs; otherwise you agree to live with, and be the source of, constant frustration. Also, if you have an employee who is not fitting in, consider letting him or her go, or transferring the person. The right fit is essential to a fun, productive workplace.

4. Indulge in guilt-free leisure

Being successful requires such commitment that professionals sometimes have a hard time turning it off. They work all day, then bring work home, and when they're not actually working, they're thinking about it. This causes stress. You can't go at it nonstop without burning out, losing your effectiveness, and possibly becoming ill. Schedule at least one waking hour just for yourself every day, and do with it whatever you wish, whether it's playing with your children, watching TV, or reading a thriller. The only rule: Don't think about work.

One day last winter during a crazy and hectic period, the two of us were feeling particularly overstressed. We decided to break from our routine of fourteen-hour days and play truant in the middle of the afternoon. Since neither of us had any pressing appointments, we skipped left and headed off to the movies for a two-hour respite. It felt wonderful to decompress and turn off our minds. (And, considering the movie was *Rocky IV*, a turned-off mind was just the ticket. What a dog!) The next time you're feeling overwhelmed by work stress, go to the movies and get into somebody else's drama.

5. Take a walk

A walk is one of the most effective stress-management tools available. A quick ten-minute walk not only gets the blood moving but lets you clear your mind as well. Feel like you want to strangle someone? Just found out about the big mistake?

Walk before you talk and you're far less likely to do or say something you'll regret. Feeling afternoon tiredness? A short walk is much better than a cup of coffee for an energy pick-me-up.

6. Say 'no way'

A constant stress that many people face is the feeling of having more to do than they can do well. Yet the pressure is always on to do more. Start saying no. Whether it's an extra project, committee assignment, or dinner date, unless it fits in with your goals, wants, and job description, politely decline. You don't have to give a reason, but you do have to be firm. If you're currently a 'yes person', it will feel odd at first, but *keep it up*. Soon people will come to respect your time. After all, the more things you say no to, the more you can say yes to.

7. Fight fair

When you run into a disagreement with someone, rather than start an argument, schedule time to 'sort it out'. You will have bought yourself some time to let any bad emotions cool, and it will be a lot easier to separate the problem from the person (see Success Shortcut 18). If you find out you were wrong, admit it with a smile and feel proud that you didn't allow your pride to harm your relationship. If the other person admits to being wrong, forgive quickly and move on. Although conflict is a major source of stress in professional life, it can be dealt with positively. Make it your goal to become comfortable with conflict, and then become good at handling it.

8. Do the one thing you must

If there's only one thing you do to manage your stress, let it be exercise. No, you're not too busy. Ride a stationary bike when you read the morning newspaper, or jog in place while you watch the evening news (it will relax you like a cocktail, yet with *positive* side effects). Take a brisk walk during lunch. Regular exercise has the mega-benefits of making your heart and lungs stronger, giving you more energy and a better self-image, letting you sleep less, and making you more attractive. You also produce some natural drugs in the process (endorphins,

your body's own painkillers, are released during heavy exercise).
Yet, for many people, exercise is absolutely the hardest thing
to stick with.

The media tell us that the Western world has been going
through a fitness craze for the past ten years. But do you really
believe it? How many people do you know who exercise every
day? Three times a week? Once a week? Lots of people have
two pairs of running shoes, workout clothes, and even skis,
but do they ever use them? It's not that people don't want to
get fit; they do — desperately. In fact, most people regularly
start exercise programmes. They just fail to stick with them.
Why? We can give you the reason in one sentence: They overdo
it and then lose interest.

Take Jimmy, for example. Until he graduated from high
school, he lived for sports. In grammar school he played sports
after school every day; in high school he lettered in three sports.
But in college the competition was above his level, and his
interest waned. He made a transition that many younger people
make, from player to spectator. After college, his career became
his excuse for not working out and staying fit. Since he did
not gain weight and still felt fine, he shrugged it off... until
he was about to turn thirty. That's when he realized that over
ten years had passed since he had done anything for his muscles
or cardiovascular system. Even though he avoided cigarettes
and alcohol, he hadn't done much more than ski a dozen days
each winter.

As the age of thirty drew closer, he knew he had to commit
to some form of exercise — just for maintenance. But he wasn't
optimistic or even the slighest bit enthusiastic. You see, it wasn't
that he hadn't tried before. He had tried, all right — too hard.

At least once a year he'd get charged up, buy a new exercise
machine (or shoes, outfit, or other equipment), use it once, and
quit. The reason: He got sick. *Literally.* Recalling his 'glory
days' of high school sports, he'd always overdo it the first time;
feel sore; get faint, headachy, or nauseated; and think, 'This
isn't worth it'. It was much easier to cling to the memory of
his high school prime than to try to recreate it. As more time
passed, the thought of doing any type of exercise grew totally
unappealing — and, in fact, even intimidating. Could he still
do calisthenics without passing out? Run a mile without stopping
halfway?

It all came to a head when he went skiing for the first time last season. After fifty yards he was so out of breath he become nauseated. Frustrated, he had to confront the fact that he was not only out of shape, he was in *bad shape*. He knew reality had replaced memories.

So now you expect the story of how he took up an exercise programme and whipped his body into superb condition? Sorry. It didn't happen. He just struggled through the ski season and continued to shun regular workouts. He'd torture his body skiing on weekends, heal during the week, and then repeat the process. It was gruelling.

But then about six months later, while listening to 'The One Minute Manager Gets Fit' audiotape programme, he heard Ken Blanchard say, 'At the very minimum, do ten push-ups and ten sit-ups each day'. Jimmy thought, 'No sweat; even I can do that'. And he did — for a month. Sit-ups and push-ups became a part of his morning routine along with showering, shaving, and getting dressed. He listened to motivational tapes to keep from getting bored. The time and energy drain was so ridiculously untaxing, he found it easy to stick with the programme.

But it didn't stop there. After a month the routine was getting too easy, and he wanted more challenge. So he started riding his exercycle and using his rowing machine while watching the morning news. He actually took the initiative to exercise *more* on his own. And now, a year later, Jimmy is reversing the trend and putting himself back in the shape he wants to be in. He's even surpassed the recommended minimum of twenty minutes of exercise three times a week.

What helped him get hooked was the minimal time and energy required at first to do just ten sit-ups and push-ups. He couldn't overdo it, as it was over almost before it had begun, and therefore he didn't dread it. The exercise programme was so simple and easy that Jimmy had no problem sticking with it for twenty-one days until it become a habit — and one he wanted.

9. Work away

When the office is getting too stressful, or the pressures and interruptions are driving you mad, a good idea is to get away from it all — as long as you take your work along. Really. Working away from the office is becoming more and more common, especially when you're working on a complex or creative project. See if your boss will let you spend a day or a morning at home or in the library. To allay any doubts the boss may have as to your productivity, make sure you show him or her the progress you made. Getting out of the office now and then can make you not only feel better, but work better. A psychiatrist we know started renting a limousine for two hours every week to do a task he hates: his billings. Now that he takes care of this work in the limousine, he says he looks forward to it.

10. Take a ten-minute sabbatical

And take one every afternoon (instead of a coffee break). It's good preventive medicine for stress. Hold your calls, sit back, take a couple of deep breaths, and let your mind travel. Go to a favourite place — a beach, a waterfall, a challenging ski slope, wherever your fantasies take you. Feel yourself becoming comfortable, content, and relaxed, then carry that feeling out of your 'sabbatical' and into your office. This technique is as powerful as it is simple. Try it. If others give you odd looks, ignore them!

11. Get a pal, be a pal

Sometimes all you need is someone to talk to, to confide in, to complain to, to cry in front of, to tell — in graphic detail — what you'd like to do to your boss after you get him or her tied down. Having somebody you can go to when you're feeling overwhelmed can ease the tension of a stressful day. There are two criteria to make this work. First, make a deal that you will give each other advice only when it's asked for, and the rest of the time you are free to say outrageous things you'll never be reminded of. Second, there must be complete trust. After you have shared enough confidences with each other, that shouldn't be too difficult.

12. Change one thing at a time

As we said in Success Shortcut 1, a primary reason people fail to make changes in their lives is that they try to do it wholesale. Don't give up smoking and drinking, change your diet, and start exercising all the same day (unless you really want to experience stress!). Select one of the stress-management tools we've presented in this chapter and practise it for three weeks — that's about the amount of time it takes to integrate a new behaviour into your daily routine. Then select another tool and repeat the process. Each new challenge feeds on past successes. Before you know it, you'll have become the calmer, more energetic and purposeful person you set out to be.

Concentrate and Increase Your Output

Learn to Burn

Concentration is my motto. First honesty,
then industry, then concentration.
                    — ANDREW CARNEGIE

Concentration is the road to reaching your highest levels of intellectual and intuitive powers. It not only increases the quantity of your output by enabling you to process information more quickly, it also increases the quality and sophistication of your ideas.

Think of an exotic car: When it's fine-tuned, warmed up and cruising, it's not only moving fast, it's running more smoothly *and* burning less fuel. Your mind operates in much the same way. When you achieve a deep level of focused thinking, you're at your best and most efficient.

Recognize the feeling? When you're concentrating you burn through work — piles of paperwork disappear, dictated letters and reports roll off your tongue, and ideas pour out of you. In this turned-on state you can accomplish in minutes what normally might take you hours.

This ability to zero in is essential to big-time success. We all know people who are so productive that we wonder how they do it. They produce enormous amounts of high-quality work, plus they're always ready with an idea. Sometimes these people are written off as workaholics. Sometimes they're seen as geniuses, with skills that deserve respect but are too far out of reach for others to acquire. The truth is that these people may simply have learned how to concentrate. While most of us see concentration as an occasional lucky accident or a gift reserved for the few, these people have treated it as a skill. They know that like all skills it can be practised and mastered.

While concentration is a high-payoff mind skill, it's one of the more difficult shortcuts to master (remember your school days, when your concentration span was ten minutes on a good study night?). The good news is the more you do it, the easier it gets — and the better the results.

THE HOW-TO-DO-ITS

1. Create the right environment
Generally, you do your concentrating in two places: your office and a workspace at home. Invest the time and effort to get these spaces set up to support, not distract, your concentration. Make sure your seating is comfortable, your lighting abundant, and your workspace clean. Get the supplies and tools you need, even if it means buying extras (don't distract yourself by rummaging through a drawer every time you need a roll of tape). Create an atmosphere that is flexible enough to support different kinds of work — for instance, a bright lamp for reading and a softer light (even candles) for more introspective work. If you are really keen, you can create two work centres: a reading/listening area where you take in information, and a writing/implementation centre where you put out information.

2. Shut the door
Even the best environment is ineffective if you can't eliminate outside distractions. A concentrative state is a very fragile thing; you must take precautions to nourish and protect it. At home that means turning off the TV and radio, turning on your answering machine (or unplugging your phone), and sending the kids to the cinema. At work, ask the receptionist or your secretary to hold your calls and prevent interruptions. If you don't have a receptionist or secretary, put a 'Do Not Disturb' sign on your door. Most of all, don't worry about missing something — the world will still be there when you open the door.

3. Send yourself to Siberia
This is the next step beyond shutting the door. It means making yourself unavailable by physically secluding yourself from the world. Jimmy remembers the times in college when he absolutely, positively had to get some studying done. He would make

those rare occasions as easy as possible by packing up his books and heading off to the sixteenth floor of the physics building. There he had discovered an out-of-the-way lecture hall where he could lock himself up and disengage from the dramas of college life. Thanks to the sixteenth floor, he graduated. An executive we know in Manhattan often has trouble concentrating on the work he brings home. His solution costs a little money but it works like a charm: He rents a hotel room for a day. What is the 'sixteenth floor' or 'hotel room' in your life? The public library, a quiet park, a rarely used conference room? Find one and use it.

4. Take a bite you can swallow

When you're all warmed up and ready to plunge into a major project, don't. Instead, take a minute to slice off a bite-sized portion you *know* you can finish in the time you have. This has a couple of advantages. First, when you set sub-goals, you can anticipate your achievement; you'll know exactly what you will accomplish in a specific time. That's always more motivating than the vague goal of 'making progress' on a project. Second, when you concentrate on a more manageable bite, it's easier for your mind to absorb the details and process the information. You won't be overwhelmed by the whole and lose your appetite.

5. Do a warm-up

You don't find athletes performing without first warming up. A warm-up is also necessary for mental athletics. The problem is that warm-ups are uncomfortable and boring: your 'muscles' are sore, your 'joints' are creaking, and it's frustrating to be stretching your hamstrings when you're psyched up for leaping the hurdles. But a warm-up *is* necessary. Say your 'In' basket is piled a foot high with papers. Ease into it, starting with short memo reading, then going on to light paperwork, and then longer reports. Depending on how 'out of shape' you are, it may take you an hour or more to hit your stride. But once you're there, it's worth it; you'll burn through even the most massive projects that earlier seemed intimidating. The willingness to endure a warm-up could very well be the one key difference between people who have great output and those who don't.

6. Practise 'focused thinking'

There are lots of ways to develop concentration: biofeedback yoga, chanting, meditation, and plain old physical exercise are all good 'centreing' techniques. Yet perhaps the most practical for your purposes is to centre your mind actively on your work. When it wanders, grab it and drag it back to the topic at hand. Don't give an inch. You may find this focused thinking brutally difficult at first, but soon your mind will get used to it. Try these concentration techniques for ten minutes (remember from Success Shortcut 4, you can do anything for ten minutes). Continue to extend this forced concentration span until you've achieved a comfortable and productive level.

7. Go with it

When you're doing well, stay with it till you drop. We mean it. When you find yourself thinking brilliant thoughts, solving problems, and writing perfect sentences, it's tempting to stop and celebrate your newfound genius. Don't! We both remember earlier in our careers when we'd be struggling on a project and then it would start to become easier. Just at the moment we would get cocky and walk away, believing we had the job in the bag. We'd tell ourselves we could come back to 'clean up the details' anytime. Unfortunately, when we returned, it sometimes took hours to get back to the mental state we had achieved, if we could get there at all. The moral: when you're on a roll, butter it (in other words, go with it).

8. Don't leave the house

Working at home is one of the simplest and best-kept secrets of high productivity. Often the complexity and pace of what's going on at the office can keep you from entering a concentrative state. That's not necessarily bad. The office is a place to implement projects and collaborate with others. It's rarely the place for the lonely task of concentration and focused thinking. We're not advocating workaholism here by saying you should work extra hours at home. In fact, you may be able to arrange to work at home during business hours. Please keep in mind, however, that most high achievers do put in at least a few extra hours of work at home per week — and it pays off for them.

9. Take advantage of being anonymous

This is another environment-related concentration technique: Make yourself invisible. It oftens happens by accident. Have you ever found yourself stranded in an airport because of a three-hour plane delay? In a waiting room for an hour because your doctor had an emergency and couldn't see you on time? At a bus or train station waiting for a friend who missed the earlier departure? These are the best times to do some hard-core concentrating, since you have absolutely nothing better to do. Always keep a pad and pen handy for such magical opportunities.

Jeff remembers writing the entire first draft of a brochure in thirty minutes while waiting in a service bay for his car to be fixed. The noise, the smells, the commotion — nothing bothered him. Because he knew not a soul, and not a soul knew him, it was easy to 'detach' and turn out some work.

10. Get in a 'same-time, same-place' habit

It's much easier to concentrate when you have to, so *force* yourself. Build time into your schedule each day to concentrate on your important goals. Here are some habits that have proven to work well for high achievers: 1 Plan a 'quiet hour' that you enforce with yourself (and others) at the same time every day. 2 Work your first hour or two every day at home. 3 Set aside a two- or three-hour block on weekends (Saturday morning or Sunday night are terrific times to concentrate). Develop a habit for yourself and stick to it. Your mind will become accustomed to it, and you will find concentrating much easier.

11. Try it before or after eight

Before eight o'clock in the morning or after eight o'clock at night, that is. Although it's good to develop a 'same-time, same-place' concentration habit, sometimes it pays to alter it. The mood to concentrate has been known to strike when it's least expected: on a Saturday night when you're at a party, at three o'clock in the morning when you're lying in bed with your mind racing. When that happens, respond. Leave the party. Get up out of bed. Go to your workspace and work. There can be something mystical about concentrating and creating while the sun is down that inspires you to react to your deepest mental state.

Besides, you weren't going to have fun at the party anyway, and you certainly weren't going to get to sleep. These moments of inspiration are rare enough; don't let them get away.

12. Love it or leave it

You know how hard it is to concentrate on a project you loathe. It's quite a challenge to keep your mind on something you hate (unless, of course, you're trying to figure out how to kill it). When you're really working well on a project, though, you don't have to straggle to concentrate. And if you love it, you can concentrate with the walls crumbling down around you. You're not distracted by the fact that you could be doing something more fun or less taxing. If you find yourself unable to concentrate because you're put off by, or apathetic about, your job, get a new job. It's just that simple. You'll never reach your potential otherwise.

Have More and Better Ideas

How to Create Creativity

Creativity is the making of the new and the rearranging of the old.
— MIKE VANCE, former Dean of Walt Disney University

Nothing happens until somebody has an idea. Creativity is one quality that separates us from animals. After all, sticks and sharp stones had been lying around for eons, but it was man who put them together to make a spear. Creativity has been the source of progress ever since.

Creativity brings payoffs on levels from the mundane to the miraculous. It's the force behind the great works of art and discoveries of science. It's the spark behind the major insight that helps you develop a new profit centre for your company. It's the curiosity that prompts you to try a new recipe. It's what you draw on to discover a way to deal with a difficult person in your life. In ways such as these, creativity constantly opens you up to new opportunities, great and small.

Having more and better ideas is essential on the job. This is especially true today, when an organization's survival and success depend on changing responses to a changing world. By developing your ability to come up wth 'new and improved' ideas, you dramatically increase your value, visibility, and upward mobility.

Another payoff to creativity is that new-idea people have more fun. They're more playful (because they know, or sense, that many good ideas come from play). They laugh more. They're more confident and self-satisfied, because they're exercising such an important part of themselves.

Like many so-called talents, creativity is often seen as a gift rather than a skill. In some ways it may be, but the good news is that this gift has been given to everyone. Every thinking, feeling human being has the capacity for creativity. Some people believe this capacity is limitless. The following ideas and activities will help you release all of the ideas, solutions, and insights you have locked inside you.

THE HOW-TO-DO-ITS

1. Think of yourself as a creative genius

One of the greatest impediments to creativity is the belief that you're not creative. Many people carry this self-concept around, in most cases because it's what they were told by their parents and teachers. They put creativity on a pedestal and look with awe at creative people. Yet a closer look reveals that even the most successful creative ideas are not magical or even particularly elusive.

Take the American, Nolan Bushnell, for instance. He invented the video game. He says the key to his invention was the realization that people like to play games and people like to watch television. He simply asked himself how he could put them together. That's not such a brilliant concept, yet Bushnell turned it into a hundred-million-dollar idea. As we have said, creativity is what makes us human, and you have been gifted with more creative potential than you will ever use. Recognize yourself for the creative genius you are and you will be able to put your creativity to use more effectively.

2. Listen to your inner voice

The subconscious mind is often at work on a problem while the conscious mind is off doing something else, like sleeping or enjoying itself. Develop a conscious relationship with your subconscious mind. When insights hit, drop everything and turn your attention to them. Write them down immediately. Messages from your inner voice are something like dreams; as vivid as they are when they happen, they fade very rapidly.

Adding to the mystery — and the urgency — is the fact that insights, even major ones, often arrive whole. Mozart once said, 'Nor do I hear in my imagination the parts successively, but I hear them, as it were, all at once. What a delight this is I cannot tell.' To quote the poet Percy Bysshe Shelley: 'One after another the greatest writers, poets and artists confirm the fact that their work comes to them from beyond the threshold of consciousness.'

3. Break out of your patterns

Human beings love repetition. We are drawn to rhythms in music and patterns in the visual world. Our natural inclination when faced with a problem is to look at what has worked before. This tendency is the very basis of learning. Without it, even simple tasks would entail endless trial and error. It is also a trap, however, because we tend to go with the tried and true instead of *creating* other solutions. Breaking out of your comfortable, familiar patterns is one of the major principles of creativity.

One of the time-honoured ways of doing this is to put your problem on paper — but this time don't write it, draw it. Drawing engages the right hemisphere of the brain, while writing engages the left (and why use half your brain when you can use it all?). Let yourself go wild with your drawing. Chart your problem, illustrate different aspects of it with animals, turn it into a motion picture in your mind. When you bring your visual, perceptual brainpower to bear on creative problem-solving, you'll be surprised how often and easily the 'ah-ha' light flashes on. So the next time your boss catches you doodling, just tell him that you're breaking out of your normal thought patterns, and that Jimmy and Jeff said it was OK!

4. Change your scene

Sometimes that's all it takes to snap yourself into a more creative mode. Many of our best pieces have been written on airplanes. The anonymity of sitting with strangers and the feeling of flying eight miles above the earth combine to put us in a most creative frame of mind. Try it yourself, by driving home a different way from work, renting a hotel room to work on an important project, or just taking a walk in the country for the purpose of making a major decision. This may seem too easy, but it's surprisingly effective.

5. Find the second (or third) right answer

Our culture has conditioned us always to look for the right answer. Think of the tens of thousands of test questions you have answered in your years of school that had one, and only one, right answer. This has very effectively stifled creativity, because the first answer we come up with is often the most common and proven one, and therefore the least creative. Many people, upon finding an answer to a problem, immediately breathe a sigh of relief and say, 'That sounds good; let's go with it'. People who are more creative, and usually more successful, will generally respond to a right answer by saying, 'That's a good answer; now let's see if we can find something better or different'.

One good way to generate lots of alternative answers is to route what we call 'plussing memos'. When you have a problem, write it up in a short memo with *all* the facts and *all* the possible solutions you can think of. Then route it to all the people you feel might have an opinion on how to solve the problem, and request their feedback. Don't limit yourself to people in your department or upper management; lower-level office staff can often give you surprisingly good solutions. By soliciting input from a variety of sources, you'll always get at least a couple of ideas you hadn't considered.

6. Learn to play the violin

A young man once asked Peter Drucker how to become a better manager. 'Learn how to play the violin,' Drucker replied. We don't think Mr. Drucker wanted that statement to be taken literally. He was just suggesting that any activity which puts you in a different context or forces you to operate outside your comfort zone will increase your creativity. The best activities are those that utilize the side of the brain you don't normally favour. Sometimes these complementary activities form a marriage made in heaven, and we find artists who are master chess players, and business people who are virtuoso musicians.

7. Argue the other side

It helps your creativity to hold your strongest core beliefs up to scrutiny periodically. Ask yourself, 'What are the *advantages* of communism?' 'Must I *always* be polite?' If you chair the committee to abolish capital punishment, try arguing *for* capital punishment (if only to yourself). Next time you are about to say, 'I can't resist chocolate', say instead, 'I *can* resist chocolate'.

This exercise may cause you to commit to your original idea all the more strongly. On the other hand, it may cause you to adjust your idea, or abandon it completely, which opens you up to a world of new ideas to examine and use. As Roger von Oech, author of the best-selling creativity book *A Whack on the Side of the Head*, says,'I think one of life's great thrills is falling out of love with a previously cherished idea'. (NB: We're not communists, we're very polite, we differ on capital punishment, and neither of us can resist chocolate!)

8. Relax the critical part of the brain

It's almost impossible to be creative when you're *trying* to be creative. To really let the ideas flow, you have to suppress any critical, acquisitive, desperate-for-an-idea attitudes you may have. Ideas can't be forced, they can only unfold on their own power. That's why it's easy to be creative about things for which you are passionate. To be creative it is necessary to call up the right attitudes or brain state. We will look at several ways to do this in the next few points.

9. Believe that a solution is possible ..

... and that you will find it. This is another way to take off the pressure and free your mind to create. Sometimes when faced with a problem, you may experience your confidence waning. You ask yourself, 'Am I really up to this?' 'Are these ideas any good?' 'I don't know the first thing about this problem'. At this point, your mind is more wrapped up in the problem than the solution. Snap out of it. Accept as if by faith that there is a solution, and that every step you take, every calculation you make, and every word you write will take you closer to it.

10. Formalize brainstorming

Brainstorming is a classic approach to generating ideas. A group of people (preferably five to eight) meet, address a problem, and come up with as many ideas and solutions as they can. The key is to suspend criticism. In brainstorming, recognize and record every idea, no matter how offbeat or off-base. This frees the mind to move into new territory without fear. When all the ideas are exhausted and the flip charts are full, the group can critically review each idea. (Hint: Allow each person to critique each idea alone first. It's a good way to encourage further creativity and minimize group-think.)

At CareerTrack we have formalized the brainstorming meeting. Every Friday morning at 7.30 a.m. (nice and early so as not to interrupt the normal work day), a group of people meet to brainstorm an issue. To make it easier to get up early and arrive on time, we serve breakfast. In the first fifteen minutes, the initiator, usually the person behind the issue under discussion, presents the background of the project, while the others eat their breakfast. Then, for the next forty-five minutes, it's a free-for-all forum where anyone can toss out an idea, while notes are frantically taken. We use these brainstorming meetings primarily to launch new ideas and products, but we'll occasionally get together to search for creative solutions to problems.

Another technique we use at CareerTrack to generate more and better ideas is contests. We've found them to be a fun and effective way to mobilize a hundred minds on a creative search for solutions. Here's an example. In the early days of our company, when the two of us were trying to come up with a slogan to support our company name (like 'Coke: The Real Thing'), we just couldn't seem to think of one which reflected our true identity and purpose. After rejecting all of our own slogans as 'not quite right', we decided to ask our people to help via a contest. The deal was this: whoever came up with the winning line (they couldn't submit unlimited entries) would receive a gift certificate to the Flagstaff House (Boulder's finest restaurant) and a cheque for $200. We received a mass of suggestions, and from them we selected our theme line, 'CareerTrack: Your Success Company'. The contest approach enabled us to tap the minds of all our employees, make them feel a part of the creative process, and choose from scores of options. Plus, we had a good time dramatizing the outcome when we announced the winner at our staff meeting amidst lots of excitement, cheering, and noise. Next time you need creative assistance, have a contest!

11. Be a nightwriter

As inconvenient as it is, this is when many of your best ideas will come — if you let them. Creative people consistently report that major insights 'hit' them just as they were about to fall asleep or just after they awoke. Actually, it's a matter of scientific fact: creativity is associated with theta brain waves, which predominate in the twilight area before and after deep sleep (meditation, deep breathing, and biofeedback also generate theta waves). Make it easy to take advantage of these high-quality inspirations by keeping a note-pad, tape recorder, or dictation machine beside your bed. And don't be afraid of getting up and working with the ideas. The next day you'll find the high of having been creative more than compensates for the lack of sleep.

12. Turn your ideas into action

The best payoff and reinforcement for creativity is to see its results. That's why you must take an active stance with your ideas. You probably know people who have brains full of terrific notions, yet they never seem to get around to using them. Remember, if there's one principle that gets to the core of success, it's this one: it's not what you know, it's what you do with what you know that counts. Put your ideas into practice relentlessly. See what works and what doesn't, and you'll not only exert a more positive influence on the world, you'll have more and better ideas in the future.

Make Good Decisions Quickly

The Power of Decisiveness

In a life where death is the hunter,
my friend, there is no time for fear or
regrets — only decisions.
— DON JUAN, TALES OF POWER

As strange as it may sound, in professional life it's usually more important to be decisive than it is to be right. This is one breach of logic that has been paying off for great leaders throughout history. While there are good decision-makers who are not good leaders, there are no good leaders who are not good decision-makers. Let's look at how this works.

First of all, decisiveness inspires support. Let's face it, most people are not leaders. Most people are more than happy to follow someone who looks like he or she knows the way.

Second, decisiveness intimidates the opposition. When you come down quickly and confidently on one side of an issue, it unnerves potential opponents. They wonder if you know something they don't; they see you as a formidable foe. As a result, they often will look elsewhere for a battle to fight. Also, when you make decisions quickly, you get it over with. You feel in control. The nagging anxiety of unfinished business is eliminated (and replaced with the acute anxiety of 'My God, what have I done?' Just kidding!).

Actually, a not-so-great decision made quickly can have better results than a good decision made slowly. Usually movement in any direction brings a new perspective that makes the right decision obvious. The fact is, in leading companies experimentation is replacing analysis as the decision-making process of choice. Why? *It works better.*

It's been estimated that 80 per cent of the business decisions you're faced with should be made on the spot, 15 per cent need to mature, and 5 per cent need not be made at all. Think about that when facing the many questions that cross your desk every day.

THE HOW-TO-DO-ITS

1. Know that you might blow it

Every decision is a risk, and that means you might fail. If you make it your only goal not to fail, you're going to have a very hard time making decisions. Even worse, there's no payoff for your agony; the decisions you finally make will probably be no better than if you had made them quickly. As Peter Drucker says, 'People who *don't* take risks generally make about two big mistakes a year. People who *do* take risks generally make about two big mistakes a year.' So when you blow it (and there will be times when you make a mess of things), learn everything you can from it, and then *don't do that again!* Remember, if you're not failing occasionally, you're not taking enough risks.

2. Know that you can change your mind

This one revelation alone can take much of the anxiety out of decision-making. Most decisions are not only adjustable but revocable. When facing a decision, accept the fact that you can't know for sure. Present your decisions in the spirit of 'let's try this' (say it decisively). Then if events go awry, you can change or adjust your decision (do it decisively) without sacrificing your credibility. Taking risks *and* knowing when to cut your losses is a great combination in business.

3. Don't get hung up on fact-finding

Remember the 'paralysis of analysis'? The problem stems from our formal schooling, where we were given facts and then tested on them. Once again, that which works in school fails in life. In business you almost never have enough information to make a decision. You have to dig for facts, and even then you're often not sure you can trust them. But decisions must be made anyway. So don't get hung up on the impossible task of 'getting all the facts'. Just think about the Pareto Principle: 20 per cent of the facts are critical to 80 per cent of the outcome.

4. Respect your hunches

Intuition is back in style. In fact, these days top managers take it quite seriously. Hunches are not random, *they're a result of accessing the vast knowledge and experience in your subconscious mind*. When something 'looks right' but 'feels wrong', or vice versa, it's a sign to pay close attention. Keep a mental record of the decisions you base on gut feelings and calculate your success rate. This will help you see when and where your hunches paid off, and give you the insight and confidence to act on them in the future.

5. Check your values

This is another way of using the power of the gut feeling. Ask yourself the following questions: Does this decision reflect what I know to be right? If more people made this decision, would the world be better or worse? Will this decision bring me more money, or self-respect, or both? The answers to these questions should help you to reach not only a fast decision, but also a 'right' one.

6. Ask around

Ask your associates, boss, and friends what they think of your decision. As long as you can formulate an independent judgement and take responsibility for it, you can only be helped by knowing the opinions of others. When soliciting other opinions, though, be careful not to broadcast your own. Just present the facts and issues, and let others tell you what they would do. And always remember, you have the final responsibility for every decision you make.

7. Then ask the experts

In serious matters, when there's a lot on the line, don't take a chance on a rushed decision. A quick call to your laywer, mentor, accountant, or other professional advisor could bring to light information that will make the right decision clear. Yes, it will take a little longer and might cost a bit more, but you'll minimize your risk. Inexperienced business people some-times resist going to experts, because they like to think they know everything they need to know to their jobs. But in today's complex business world, seasoned executives know how to build — and use — a trusted team of experts.

8. Go on a solution search

Pull out a note-pad, get in your creative mode (see Success Shortcut 9), and list every solution, no matter how extreme, that comes to mind. This is another way of drawing on your unconscious wisdom. When the flow of options starts to slow down, push a little further. Then stop. Switch into your critical mode and evaluate each possible decision. You may be surprised to see that one of your extreme options is clearly your best one.

9. Calculate your risk extremes

Clear your mind of all the middle ground and go right for the extremes. Think of the best and the worst possible outcome of your decision. How much can you afford to put on the line? If you see that you have a high-upside, low-downside risk (otherwise known as a lot to gain and little to lose), then go for it. If you see that you have a low-upside, high-downside risk, then be more conservative. In many cases this is all you'll have to do to make a good, quick decision.

10. Let someone else decide

We're not suggesting you hand it to someone else and say, 'Here, *you* decide'. You can't delegate the ultimate responsibility, but you can delegate most of the work. We remember when we had to select between two phone systems that appeared to be equal in quality and options. We urgently needed to decide, but neither of us had the time to research and compare the systems properly. So we delegated the job to our head receptionist and senior computer analyst. The receptionist evaluated the user-friendliness of the systems, while the analyst looked at cost, growth potential, and compatibility with the current system. That left financing and company reputation for us to examine. We made the decision in two weeks and it was a good one. Even better, two key people had 'ownership' in the decision and, therefore, fully supported its implementation. In fact, now that the system is installed, they are responsible for keeping it in proper working order.

11. Refuse to decide

There's nothing more decisive than stating, 'I'm not going to decide this right now'. The key is to gauge the consequences of waiting. When waiting incurs a high-downside risk — as it did when the captain of the *Titanic* heard reports of icebergs — decide immediately (incidentally, he didn't). When there's a low-downside risk to waiting, however, some decisions can be improved by delay. For instance, if you have two subordinates in conflict who want you to decide who's 'right', it may pay to wait till tempers have cooled.

12. Grow a decision tree

Thinking of changing jobs? Getting married? Firing someone? Every now and then you're faced with 'the big one', a decision you want to make right the first time. In these cases, a quick decision is probably not the best. The decision tree is a classic exercise that lets you evaluate your options statistically. It is often promoted as a good basic tool, which it isn't; it's far too cumbersome for routine decision-making. Yet when the consequences are major, a decision tree can serve you well. For detailed instructions on how to construct a decision tree, see the book *Management Tools for Everybody*, which appears in the bibliography on page 259.

Listen
Aggressively

Hear What People Are Saying

*A good listener is not only popular everywhere,
but after a while he knows something.*
— WILSON MIZNER

'What?'
'I never said that'.
'I'm sorry, what was your name again?'
'Nobody ever tells me what's going on around here'.
'That's not my understanding of our agreement'.
'Oh, bother, I forgot'.
'I see what you mean now, but I *thought* you meant . . .'

What we have here is a failure to communicate. And in every case it was caused by a failure to listen. In most organizations the cost of this failure is staggering — in wasted time, lost opportunities, and strained relationships. Like most people, you may think listening is passive, that you can't control or improve it. But you can, by listening aggressively. What do we mean by listening 'aggressively'? We mean forcing yourself to concentrate on every word, questioning, cutting in (gently, of course), or asking for clarification. Sometimes you have to take charge of a conversation even when you're not the one doing the talking. Make it your own private game: don't let the speaker get away until you understand every detail of what he or she is saying. When a point is not clear, speak up and get clarification. In the process you will gain communication powers you've never had before.

- *You'll reduce mistakes and misunderstandings.* Good listening skills let you get the story straight the first time.
- *You'll save time*, by getting people to come to the point quickly and clearly.
- *You'll improve your concentration and memory.* Listening skills help you absorb and retain more information, retrievable at will.

- *You'll get more information from people*, by learning to 'listen' to their non-verbal cues. This includes information they may have forgotten or are leaving out.
- *You'll discover that others are more responsive to you.* As Thoreau said, "The greatest compliment that was ever paid me was when someone asked me what I thought, and attended to the answer." Listening is one of the most powerful people skills. By really listening to people you make them feel more important. They're more likely to trust you and open up to you, making your relationships stronger.
- And finally, *you'll make more sales*, whether you're selling products or ideas. The one timeless truism of sales is 'Listen to what people want, then give it to them'.

Obviously listening effectively can lead to substantial payoffs. Here are twelve ways to be a better listener and cash in.

THE HOW-TO-DO-ITS

1. Consciously concentrate

One of the biggest barriers to listening is that most of us have learned *not* to listen. It's a matter of survival; there is so much racket in the world we have to be selective as to what we give our attention to. And since 'tuning out' has become such a natural and comfortable habit, we sometimes forget to tune back in again, even when we need to. So when you enter a situation where you know you have to listen, put yourself — forcibly, if necessary — into a 'tuned-in' mode. Bear down, suppress other thoughts, and focus. It may be simple, but it works.

2. Visibly respond to the speaker

Another natural inclination as a listener is to race around the speaker: to jump to tangential ideas, prepare a response, or mentally criticize what he or she is saying. Unfortunately, while you are preoccupied with your own ruminations, the speaker may race ahead of you. The solution is to respond to the speaker every step of the way. Act interested. Maintain eye contact (if you find your eyes drawn away, your mind won't be far behind). Also, demonstrate your interest by nodding, saying 'uh-huh', and adopting an alert, tuned-in posture. Let the speaker know you care. He or she is far more likely to tell you what you need to know — and you are more likely to hear it.

3. Don't talk when you're listening

It's like talking with your mouth full: rude. Many so-called conversations are more like alternating monologues. There's a difference between listening and just waiting for your turn to talk! Many people become such insensitive listeners that they chronically interrupt. Although interrupting can be appropriate at times (see point 7), it is a subtle power play and often leaves the other person feeling discounted. Closeness, rapport, and commitment are killed.

4. Create informal situations

In informal situations people open up more readily and reveal their true personalities, instead of their facades. The power of an informal situation became clear to Jeff a couple of years ago when he was interviewing a job applicant for CareerTrack. It was an important position so, naturally, Jeff wanted to hire the best person possible for the job. One of the top candidates, Nancy, came to Jeff's office for an interview, and he liked her right away. The 'chemistry' was good, she had an impressive portfolio, and she'd worked for another company for several years, proving her loyalty.

Unfortunately, in the interview Nancy was immobilized by nervousness. Her mouth was dry, and she sat like a statue and stared at the floor. Jeff tried every technique he knew to help her relax: he came around from behind his desk, smiled, made jokes — none of it worked.

After about ten minutes of tortured questions and answers, he said, 'OK, Nancy, if there's nothing else, let's just call it an interview. I'll let you know my decision in a couple of days'. She agreed to that (with a silent nod, as Jeff recalls) and gathered up her portfolio. Jeff escorted her into the hall. 'You know', he said, 'this interviewing is a real pain in the neck, isn't it?'

'Yes!' she said with an explosive sigh. 'You don't know what it's like, going around from company to company with my little satchel, showing my work for people to criticize. It's awful!' Jeff answered sympathetically, 'I *do* know. I used to do it, too.'

As they continued walking and talking, Nancy told Jeff what she really wanted from a job and what she could offer in return. Her career was of central importance in her life, and she was quite enthusiastic about contributing her best to the right organization. Jeff accompanied her all the way to the parking lot, where they leaned against her car and continued talking another fifteen or twenty minutes. This after-the-interview conversation was more honest, candid, and revealing than any job interview Jeff had ever conducted. The point is, although Nancy was paralysed by the formality of the job interview, she was able to converse naturally in an informal setting. Jeff had responded to her and had created a situation (however unintentionally) in which she could be herself. (By the way, Nancy still works at CareerTrack.)

5. Don't filter out the negative

The good news is that when we listen to what we want to hear, we're all ears. The bad news is that when we hear something that goes against our wishes or assumptions, we tune out entirely. For instance, suppose a colleague tells you, 'I'll have that project done by Wednesday if all the materials come in'. Because you want the project completed by Wednesday, you latch on to the first part of the statement and make your plans accordingly. It's not until Wednesday — when the project isn't done, because the materials didn't come in — that you remember *everything* that was said. By then it's too late.

Jimmy has an amusing anecdote to illustrate the dangers of filtering. One evening when he was dining at a favourite Italian restaurant, the waiter served Jimmy an inedible appetizer that contained enough garlic to asphyxiate everyone in the room. The waiter eventually came by and asked the standard question: 'How is everything?' Jimmy replied, 'Since you asked, not so good. It seems there's been a mistake here', and he explained the problem. Naturally, another appetizer was brought to him, and the dinner went on.

Later, the owner of the restaurant came to the table and apologized, offering Jimmy a dessert on the house. Jimmy was pleased and thought, 'Wow, these people are serious about customer service and quality control.'

A top-drawer restaurant, right? Well ... three months later Jimmy was in the same restaurant, when he observed the head chef walking through the dining room, stopping by each table to ask the diners how they were enjoying their meals. As the chef moved from table to table, they would smile and nod, and he would say, 'Thank you very much'. Finally he got to Jimmy. Jimmy wouldn't have gone out of his way to complain, but since the chef *did* ask, he said, 'To tell you the truth, my meal is a little cold'.

Well, the customer service wasn't so hot that night. The chef just smiled and said, 'Thank you very much', and kept right on going. Now *that's* filtering out the negative!

6. Sum up

This is particularly valuable in those situations where you absolutely have to understand what is said. When the speaker comes to a natural pause after finishing a point, paraphrase what he or she has said. This will not only help to crystallize the ideas in your mind, but it will give the speaker the opportunity to clear up anything that was miscommunicated. It also aids memory. When it's not possible to sum up aloud — such as at a conference or seminar — do it in your head or take notes.

7. Interrogate — politely

The best technique for aggressive listening is asking questions, which is particularly effective with people who ramble. It makes them realize you are serious about gaining information and will not indulge their sloppy communication style. If you're dealing with a rambler, feel free to interrupt occasionally (politely, of course) with a question; it forces the speaker to come to the point. Questioning also works with shy or inarticulate people. Knowing that *you* — the listener — have taken charge of the conversation makes it easier for them to talk. It also makes them feel more important, which gives them the confidence to speak better.

8. Take notes, but not too many

It can be difficult to listen and write simultaneously, but often it is essential, especially in business, to remembering what was said. The pitfall, of course, is that you may be too busy writing to keep up with what's being said. The trick is to take selective notes: get down key words, phrases, and statistics. When writing notes, try not to be too conspicuous; the speaker could be intimidated by your 'taking down' every word he or she says.

9. Refuse to listen

In those instances where a speaker is talking miles over your head or is hopelessly incoherent, often the best response is simply not to lend your ear. Why spend time being bored or frustrated when you could be getting the information from a better source? Life is too short to spend it stifling yawns and feigning attention because a speaker didn't take the time, or doesn't have the skill, to make himself or herself understood. It's up to you; in each situation you have to calculate the value of listening versus the consequences of not listening.

10. Don't kill the messenger

Sometimes people — particularly busy, task-oriented people (like bosses) — fly off the handle when they hear bad news. Are you ever guilty of this reaction? If you want people to cover up problems and keep the hard facts from coming to the surface, this is a great technique. If, on the other hand, you want to be kept abreast of the information you need to do your job, stay cool. In fact, welcome and reward the delivery of bad news as you would that of good news. It's just as valuable to you.

This applies to all areas of business. One major new idea in management technique is to listen to — and even solicit — bad news not only from employees (see Confidential Feedback Form on page 195 and Reverse Performance Appraisal on page 198) but from customers as well. Tom Peters, co-author of *In Search of Excellence* and guru of excellence-oriented management, advocates systematizing the process of listening to bad news from customers by, strangely enough, calling them up and talking with them. He calls it 'getting your daily dose of reality'.

At CareerTrack we have created a form around the idea;

we use it regularly, in personal conversations with our customers, to find out just how we're perceived. As in any face-to-face critique, most people will try to be nice. You must encourage your customers to give you the bad with the good. And then, of course, you have to *do something about it*. Figure 11.1 is a stereotyped version of our dose of reality form which you can adapt or use.

Notice that the text is very conversational. This is important, because the purpose of the form is not to 'conduct a survey' but to *have a free-flowing conversation with a customer*. Use the script only as a general guideline; let the conversation go in any direction (consider this your chance to use all your listening skills). You'll often get your best information and insights as a result of questions you had no original intention of asking. If you're lucky you'll get an earful.

11. Get to yes or no

Sometimes you need a quick answer, without all the details. When you're under this kind of pressure, simply say, 'Can you tell me this: Is it yes or no?' If that feels a little abrupt to you, try: 'Is it *mostly* yes or *mostly* no?' Another method of speeding up an answer is to ask a speaker to give you 'in twenty-five words or less' a summation of the facts you need.

12. Listen to more than the words

Research shows that 93 per cent of a speaker's message is communicated non-verbally, through tone of voice and body language. Much of this message is received and processed unconsciously (although you're unaware of it, your brain makes hundreds of calculations per second). When you're listening to someone, consider his or her posture, intonation, facial expressions, and gestures to find what is really being said. Trust your intuition and gut feeling. If a message sounds right yet feels wrong, a red flag has been raised. Look and listen a little closer.

Your Name _____

MY DOSE OF REALITY

Customer's name _____
Company _____
Address _____ Phone _____
Product/Service _____
Date Bought/Served _____
Server/Salesperson/Contact _____

SCRIPT:

'Hello, (their name), this is (your name) from (your organization). On (date) you (bought, used, attended, etc.) a (product, service) from us. I'm calling to see how you like(d) it, and what feedback you might be able to give us so we can serve you better in the future. Can I have three minutes of your time?'

'How did you like the (product, service)?' (Was it what you expected, is it working as planned, etc.?)

_____

_____

'How about the (delivery/server/salesperson/contact)?' (Were they courteous, knowledgeable, competent, etc.?)

_____

_____

'Is there anything about your dealings with our organization that annoyed you?'

_____

_____

'Do you have any advice for us? What else could we be doing to serve you better?'

_____

_____

FOLLOW-UP

☐ Written note thanking customer for time and ideas.

☐ Additional follow-up for customer (problem to solve, etc.):

_____

_____

☐ Your insights and/or actions as a result of this call:

_____

_____

Figure 11.1   'Dose-of-reality' form

Conduct Meetings That Get Results

Maximize Your Meetings

Many meetings should not occur at all.
— R. ALEC MACKENZIE, *THE TIME TRAP*

How often have you sat for over an hour in a meeting that was going nowhere? Witnessed two associates as giving over a meaningless point? Listened to a speaker talk forever and say nothing? Felt the anxiety of wondering, 'Why am I sitting here when I could be *doing* something?'

It doesn't have to be this way. Although meetings are usually high on most professionals' lists of timewasters, the fact is they can constitute some of the most productive time you spend.

There are five basic purposes for a meeting: 1 to disseminate information; 2 to solve problems; 3 to plan; 4 to brainstorm; 5 to motivate. Many meetings will combine these purposes, although one is generally dominant. Here are the benefits of each:

1. *To disseminate information* — A meeting lets you 'get the word out' to a lot of people at one time. In many companies a system of consecutive directors' meetings, managers' meetings, and department meetings is the key means of getting information from the top to every corner of the company.

2. *To solve problems* — When two heads are better than one, then six or eight are, in most cases, better yet. When everyone who is involved in a particular problem gets together in one room, solutions evolve quickly. It's usually best to limit the size of problem-solving meetings to about eight people. More than that tends to be unwieldy and counterproductive.

3. *To plan* — By gathering all the project players at one table, a synergy occurs that transforms ideas into practical and feasible goals. Plus, you achieve a public commitment to accomplishing these goals.

4. *To brainstorm* — Meetings are the classic (and still

the best) way to generate profitable ideas or to build on somebody's 'What if?' idea.

5. *To motivate* — We all need a shot in the arm at times. A meeting is the perfect place to get your team, department — even company — psyched up for a big project, a new sales record, or a fresh commitment.

One sure sign of a well-managed company is well-run meetings, whether they are very formal (like an annual stockholders' meeting) or very informal (an encounter by the coffee machine, for instance — impromptu huddles like this can be as productive as formal meetings). But whatever the tone, the special magic is in the face-to-face interaction between people. Utilize these next twelve tips and all your future meetings will get results that will make you glad you got together.

THE HOW-TO-DO-ITS

1. Know why you're there

What *exactly* are you trying to accomplish? Why? By when? Where? With whom? Given the high cost of people's time, it's essential to have a goal in mind when you call a meeting. If there's no clear reason to meet, don't. If there is, make sure everyone knows it before you convene.

2. Write an agenda of your purpose

Many meetings, particularly regular, informal meetings, suffer for lack of a written agenda. With an agenda you always know where you're heading, what you've covered, and, just as important, when you're done. It could be anything from a simple list of points you want to cover to a typed schedule of topics, goals, and time allotments. If possible (and it generally is), see that everyone gets a copy *before* the meeting. That way they can think about the issues and bring any necessary information to the meeting. Writing an agenda takes a few minutes but will save a lot of time and energy in the long run.

The Department Meeting Agenda Organizer shown in Figure 12.1 was developed by Jimmy in the early days of CareerTrack, when he first started holding meetings. Tired of showing up unprepared and forgetting to bring up important issues, he created this form to help himself get ready to conduct a meeting. Try it for the next meeting you lead. Each Monday put a copy on your desk or in your briefcase and make notes throughout the week of items you want to cover. The 'item triggers' at the top of the form will help jog your memory for what's happened recently. If, like Jimmy, you're not one to spend time writing detailed agendas, this quick and easy organizer will ensure that you're at least prepared to cover the critical issues. Adapt it or create your own; it's a short-cut that works.

DEPARTMENT MEETING AGENDA ORGANIZER

Meeting Date: _____

ITEM TRIGGERS

- Employees/Suppliers/Customers
- Products/Services
- Procedures/Systems
- Office Changes
- Progress on Current Projects

- Personnel Issues/Policy Changes
- Outstanding Accomplishments
- Doses of Reality/Points of Irritation
- Special Upcoming Events
- Handouts (articles, form, etc.)

1.   6.

2.   7.

3.   8.

4.   9.

5.   10.

Figure 12.1   Department Meeting Agenda Organizer

3. Let someone lead

A group without a leader will probably get no results. Someone has to be in charge of preparing the agenda, keeping the meeting moving, and ensuring something is achieved. The chair person of the meeting should not necessarily be the person of highest rank, but rather the person who 'owns' the issue to be discussed. Considering the five purposes of meetings mentioned earlier will make the appropriate person obvious: 1 information dissemination — the person with the info; 2 problem-solving — the person with the problem; 3 brainstorming — the person in need of ideas; 4 planning — the project leader; 5 motivation — the leader of the pack.

4. Enforce ground rules of openness, frankness and confidentiality

This is particularly valuable in problem-solving meetings, where sensitive issues and egos may be involved. As a chair person you must encourage straight talk, with no dancing around issues, no excuses, and no omitted evidence. Don't waste people's time with fuzzy facts. Don't condone defensiveness or scapegoating either. Encourage people to be open to change and unconventional solutions. Finally, enforce strict confidentiality, so people feel free to tell it like it is. You'll get results in hard-hitting meetings if you create a feeling of 'anything goes, and everything stays, within these walls'.

5. Keep it moving

People in groups have a frustrating habit of getting hung up on trivial points or a lack of consensus. If you feel progress stalling just say, 'Let's get back to this later in the meeting', or schedule another time to discuss it. Even a *short* break will often end a deadlock. Also, while people must feel free to express their opinions, the skilful chair person senses how to control digression and monologues, and when to move on.

A tried-and-true strategy for effective meetings is to allot a specific length of time. It provides an implicit pressure to keep things moving. This does not mean you shouldn't change your time schedule occasionally. When your group is really focused, or making progress you haven't seen in a long while, *keep going!* Don't kill a creative and collaborative discussion for the sake of punctuality. And, of course, never feel obligated to fill an alloted meeting time period after the goals are accomplished.

6. Munch

Another way to keep a meeting moving is to keep people eating. At CareerTrack's marketing meetings, somebody generally brings a huge bag of popcorn. All through the meeting, the bag travels up and down the conference table, with people grabbing handfuls and shoving it in their mouths as it passes by. Every now and then, somebody brings caramel corn, otherwise known at CareerTrack as 'bad-karma corn'. Other times the main bill of fare is jelly beans. In this case everyone scrambles to snatch up the red ones (cherry, not cinnamon). The popcorn and candy add a dimension of fun and sharing, which, in turn, promotes collaboration and teamwork. Try bringing some snacks to your next meeting.

If caramel corn and jelly beans seem a little too frivolous for your meetings, you might consider a more formal luncheon meeting. If you have an appropriate dining room in your company you could have the luncheon catered. This can lend just the right air of importance and elegance to the assembly. Or follow the more conventional approach and hold your meeting in a restaurant. Just make sure the restaurant is quiet and well run, so the dining experience adds to, rather than detracts from, the overall effect. Many executives establish a relationship with one particular restaurant to assure they'll get the finest service. It makes a great impression to meet in a restaurant where you are known by name, you get the best table or dining room, and all bills are taken care of discreetly.

7. Brush up on your one-liners

Meetings provide one of the best places to have a laugh. When people who are open and comfortable with each other get intense over an issue, a natural humour generally comes out. Enjoy it; it is necessary comic relief to the serious business at hand. A good laugh seems literally to 'shake up' a group, breaking the barriers and opening the members to new ways of thinking. It's true. Research shows that groups who laugh get almost twice as much done as groups who don't. So polish your one-liners.

When someone presents a breakthrough idea at one of our brainstorming meetings, it's become an old joke for someone else to use the line, 'OK, it's less work, we'll have it quicker, and it costs less — let's not do it!' This one-liner *always* gets a laugh — at a CareerTrack meeting, anyway.

8. Go roundtable

This is a meeting where you go around the table and give every-one a chance to talk. It's a particularly helpful way to approach weekly department or update meetings. Each person does two things: firstly, reports on progress since the last meeting, and secondly, commits to what he or she is going to do by the next meeting. A side benefit of this approach is that people tend to promise a lot in front of their peers, which maintains a healthy performance pressure (freeing the chair person from a typical taskmaster role). A quick roundtable can also be an effective ending to any kind of meeting. It gives everyone the floor to update the group, get their questions answered, or talk about whatever is on their mind.

9. Follow it up in writing

Yes, only written notes will do. Always have someone take notes on the key points discussed at every regular or important meeting (a good 'rule of thumb' is 'dollars, deadlines, and decisions'). Then have the notes typed and distributed to all concerned within twenty-four hours, and preferably within one or two hours. Format the notes as a to-the-point action plan of who will do what by when, as established at the meeting. And keep it to one page; people are far more likely to read one page than two or more.

10. Huddle

The length or formality of a meeting may have nothing to do with the quality of work accomplished. When you need to meet just for a quick decision, announcement, or update, a 'huddle' is the perfect format. Huddles take place in offices, hallways, and even parking lots. They work best when you have specific issues to resolve, have the relevant information at hand, and are dealing with busy people. Impromptu huddles can keep momentum going on important projects between more formal meetings. If an important decision is made, it's a good idea to distribute a written action plan even after huddles. Writing and distributing notes will take a few minutes, but it will save the many minutes more usually wasted by faulty memories.

11. Meet regularly as a team

Get in the *habit* of talking to each other. Your team should meet at the same time and same place each week (or more often) just to 'take care of business'. A little bit of everything happens at a good weekly department meeting: information is conveyed, problems are solved, plans made, new ideas discussed, and pep talks delivered. In fact, you can encourage people to save up issues for these meetings, which eliminates a lot of interruptions and distractions throughout the week. Everybody's issues are handled at one time. This type of meeting enables your department to feel 'whole' at least once a week, in a controlled environment with no phonecalls or interruptions. During extremely hectic times or important projects, you may decide to meet more often, even daily.

12. Meet regularly as an organization

Every company or company division should meet at least once a year for the sole purpose of letting people know what's new on the horizon and reinforcing the sense of being one group with one purpose. At CareerTrack, our entire company gathers at the end of each calendar quarter for a message from us, the company's founders. We try to put on a good show by recognizing good performers, introducing new products, reporting on the progress of current ones, and presenting policy changes. Meetings like these can — and should — be loaded with information and motivation. People leave with a renewed commitment to the company and a good sense of how they fit into the scheme of things.

Handle Mistakes and Stay Cool Under Pressure

What to Do When You Blow It

Alas, how terrible is wisdom when it
brings no profit to the man who is wise.
— SOPHOCLES

The surest way to be plagued by mistakes and problems is to try to eliminate them from your life. Yet that is exactly the stance many people take with mistakes. It's called the *everything-is-going-to-smooth-out trap*. But a mistake or problem is like a box of Christmas crackers — it always comes with a prize. That prize is either a message you needed to hear or a lesson you needed to learn. For instance, when a mistake happens in your department, consider that a red flag has been raised. A system has broken down, someone needs more training, you're understaffed. If you are a manager you need this kind of information. Don't resent it; welcome it (we know that's asking a lot), then do something about it.

If you consistently learn from mistakes in this way, then making them can actually enhance your image in your organization. Mistakes show you're trying new things. In today's organization, a person who is willing to risk making a mistake is more valuable than someone who is afraid to take action. The fact is, successful people usually make more mistakes than people who fail... but they also have more successes. They operate on the proven principle that one success can outweigh a hundred failures.

The way you handle mistakes can also make you a more respected leader. If you are able to stay cool and effective under pressure, you will invite support. You won't damage relationships by acting irrationally and behaving regrettably. 'Grace under pressure' is a rare quality, but One that you *must* develop in order to reach the top.

Also, learning to handle mistakes makes life a lot easier. By accepting mistakes and crises, *and learning from them*, you preserve your sanity. You don't waste time hiding from them and assigning blame. You develop an equanimity that puts you in tune with reality — and that not only feels better, it works better, too.

The trouble with the real world is that it's full of problems. Sometimes they are more plentiful or more difficult than at other times. Sometimes we have no control over them, and sometimes they are clearly our fault. But we will always have them. Yet many people feel that the very appearance of a problem calls their competence into question, which immediately undermines their confidence. You eliminate that danger the minute you understand that life's problems come with the territory. They do not develop because you are a bad person and deserve to be punished (well, sometimes they do), but simply because you are a human being. This is an important point, because facing a problem demands that your confidence level be at its highest. So try this: the next time you run into a problem, look at it as a challenge. Expand with excitement and confidence. Stand up to it. Stare it down. Tear it up and devour it. If that sounds like something your school football coach would say, it's because to deal with problems effectively, you really do have to accept them as wholesome challenges, and consciously and deliberately psyche yourself up.

When you can do that, you can begin to appreciate problems as valuable learning experiences, and actually welcome them into your life.

THE HOW-TO-DO-ITS

1. Remember, life has setbacks

Unfortunately, it really does. And the problem staring you in the face at this moment could be one of them. If that's the case, then deal with the situation in the most mature manner you know. Admit the failure, accept the responsibility, and bounce back as quickly as you can. Don't let a bad set of circumstances destroy you or torpedo all earlier successes. Everyone is vulner-

able to setbacks; nobody expects you not to make mistakes.
Just be sure to learn from them.

2. Buy time to clear your head

It can be hard to clear your head when everything around you
is falling apart. It takes time. If at all possible, get out of the
crisis environment. Go to the cinema, take five minutes to walk
around your building, lie down or do some relaxation exercises.
Even if you are not consciously thinking about solving your
problem, you are solving it on a level below consciousness.
Allow this process to run its course and you'll be in a far better
position to deal with your crisis.

3. Ask yourself the $64,000 question

The question is: 'What's the worst that could happen?' What
most people usually need when dealing with a mistake is a
little perspective. You can save yourself a lot of needless stress
if you realize, at the outset, that the consequences of a
catastrophe may not be all that catastrophic. At any rate, you'll
know how serious the problem is, and where you stand. Another
relevant question is: 'In five years, will it matter?' Consider:
will you be a tramp living rough in five years if you mishandle
this predicament, or will it just be a temporary setback from
which you can rebound? The answer will stop you from destroy-
ing yourself (unless, of course, the answer is yes to living rough).

4. Don't react, respond

Never panic. At the very least, never panic in public. It's simply
a matter of image. In a crisis people need to lean on someone
who is calm and seems to have the matter under control. Let
that person be you, even if you're the one who caused the
problem. If you go berserk every time something goes wrong,
you will gain a well-deserved reputation as someone who can't
take the stress.

5. Feel the pain

A major mistake or setback is a loss. And human beings have
a natural way of dealing with loss. It's called mourning. Mourning is usually associated with the loss of a loved one; but it
is also helpful in dealing with lesser losses, such as the loss

of a job or a promotion, or even the loss of esteem that comes with a major mistake. The point of mourning is simply to integrate your loss, to accept yourself and the world as being without that which you wanted, and yes, that involves feeling the pain of it. Expressing your pain is far more therapeutic than hiding from it or minimizing it (strangely enough it feels a lot better, too). Go somewhere quiet and cry your eyes out if you need to. Keep your perspective, learn your lesson, then let the pain go.

6. Find the gift

As we've noted, the best thing about a mistake is that it always comes with a gift: a lesson or an opportunity. When the two of us missed a deadline for mailing brochures in a direct-mail campaign, we were left with a couple of truckloads of worthless brochures. The event we were promoting was in three weeks, and the post office needed at least two weeks to deliver the brochures (it's suicide in our business to have just one week's lead time). This was a major, painful, costly mistake. There is nothing more worthless than dated advertising brochures. We made ourselves look for the opportunity, but what could it be?

Finally, Jimmy hit upon it: insert the brochures into the newspaper and have them delivered the next day. And it worked! It didn't work as well as if we had mailed them, but we did make a small profit (and, more important, we were saved from losing a lot of money). The point is, don't stop with the mistake. Accept as a matter of faith that there is also an opportunity, and make it your job to find it.

7. Do something, even if it's minor

Too often, particularly in crisis situations, people become immobilized. They're experiencing the bad consequences of their previous actions, and as a result, they are incapable of taking any further action. Momentarily, at least, they have lost their confidence. This is a natural phenomenon, and it must be fought. When it happens to you, get yourself moving by taking some decisive action, even if it's minor or irrelevant. Jimmy benefited from this principle on his recent vacation in Cancún, Mexico. As he tells it:

'Three weeks before I departed, while getting ready for work,

I inexplicably tore two contact lenses in less than fifteen seconds. I hadn't torn a contact lens in years, yet here I was tearing two, one after the other. So I wore my spare pair that day and made an appointment with my doctor to get replacements. Unfortunately, he had an emergency and the appointment was cancelled.

'There was no way I was going to Mexico with just one pair of contact lenses. My two vacation goals were to read and to water-ski, and I wouldn't be able to do either if something happened to the one pair of contact lenses that I had. Of course, I intended to reschedule the appointment immediately... and I intended, and I intended... until the day before I was to leave on vacation. In sudden desperation, I called and asked the doctor's assistant if I could just buy a spare pair without having to meet with the doctor. The assistant said, "Sure, but unfortunately, we don't have your prescription in stock."

"I don't believe this," I thought to myself. "I'm going to have to go and hope I don't damage or lose my *one and only pair* of contacts."

'When I got to Cancún, I decided my *special* goal was to water-ski on only one ski for the first time. I did it, no problem, on my very first try. At this point, I was getting cocky, and to tell you the truth, contact lenses were the last thing on my mind — until my next turn on the skis. Then it happened: my worst fear. The wind and spray blew my left contact lens out of my eye so fast I didn't even know what hit me. Suddenly I was half blind! Now, I'll try to find a lost contact lens in the sink, and I'll even try to find a lost contact lens on a carpet, but has anyone ever tried to find a lost contact lens in the Caribbean Sea?

'When the realization of what had happened sank in, I was filled with rage. "I knew this would happen!" I yelled at myself. "I can't believe I was so stupid as to go on a reading and skiing vacation with only one pair of contacts. My vacation is ruined!" Then I thought, "Wait a minute, you give advice on how to handle these problems. Why don't you take some of it?" So I remembered the formula: Keep calm, take action, solve first and blame later. Fighting to regain my composure, I found my way back to the office of the resort and tried to make a long-distance call to my assistant, to have her send a new pair of lenses to me. I figured I'd probably get them by the last day of my vacation, if I could even get through the phone lines. Of course I couldn't; they were jammed.

'Next door was the infirmary. I went in, only to find twelve people ahead of me, waiting for an examination so they could go scuba diving. There I was, half blind, my vacation ruined because I couldn't see or do or read a thing — and let me tell you, I was losing patience fast. I didn't care anymore about the little niceties of life such as waiting one's turn in line. I walked right up to the nurse and said, "Is there an eye doctor here?" I figured she'd roll her eyes and dismiss me and my ludicrous request. But instead she said, "Sure there is. Down in the city of Cancún," and she gave me an address.

'So I went out in front of the hotel to wait for a cab, and luck being somewhat with me at this point, one was there waiting. The driver was one of the nicest cabbies I have ever met: friendly, smiling, and helpful. He couldn't speak English very well, but I decided that gave me a chance to practise my Spanish. Positive thinking began to creep in — until the reality of my predicament once more took over. There I was, sitting in the back of a cab, thinking, "Jimmy, you know this is hopeless. You know what you really want to do is go back to your room and sulk. What are you doing out here, wandering in a blur through a strange city where you don't even speak the language?" Then, once again, I remembered what we teach: perseverance, optimism, overcoming obstacles, success goes to the activist. Newly resolved, I set my jaw — and choked on the dust coming in the passenger window.

'At last we got to the eye doctor's office. I went in and he, too, was waiting and smiling. "This is actually going to work out," I said to myself guardedly. Through some combination of pidgin Spanish and sign language, I asked him if he carried contact lenses. Well, I didn't need two years of college Spanish to understand the answer — it was no. My heart sank and I felt that rage and frustration welling up in me again. "I can't believe how stupid you've been, Jimmy, to take some rattletrap cab into this rattletrap town on some kind of wild-goose chase for a contact lens!"

'Then I looked up again. The doctor was saying something in pretty good English, and I understood him. He said, "I don't have contact lenses, but *he* does." And he pointed out of the window to another opticians across the street. "OK", I said to myself, "what's one more stop on this ill-fated journey?" So with my cabdriver (who, for some reason decided to escort me around instead of just dropping me off), I crossed the street to the other opticians' office. Once inside, I again explained my problem. "Do you have contact lenses?" I asked, "*Sí*", he answered, "what's your prescription?" I made my best guess, and what do you know, he had it! I couldn't believe my luck. "This is too easy," I thought. I was right, it *was* too easy: It was the wrong prescription.

'I was lost, I was desperate — so close yet so far away. I had no idea what my prescription was. But the doctor had a suggestion: He could examine me and find out. I looked over at the examination area in the corner of the room. Believe me, it was the antithesis of antiseptic, but I couldn't stop then. I I sat down for an examination. Within thirty seconds the doctor had determined my correct prescription, found the lens I needed, and put it in my eye. I had full vision again! My doctor in Boulder would have taken thirty minutes to do the same thing, and that would have been after I'd sat forty-five minutes in the waiting room. I couldn't believe my good fortune.

'But of course there was one last, tiny, little problem: the issue of the bill. Now, there was no way I was going to leave that doctor's office without that contact lens. And I would have paid virtually any price for the privilege of seeing for the rest of my vacation. But, naturally, I didn't want to be taken to the cleaners. And you know the stories of what happens to Americans in strange lands.

'I watched the doctor adding up the bill. "Okay, gringo," I could imagine him thinking, "now that you can see, wait till you see this!" Reluctantly I looked down at the bill. I couldn't believe my eyes; it was half of what I would have paid in the States for the same contact lens. "This really did work," I thought, "I can't believe it; it really did work!" I had passed the test. I knew that the principles of problem-solving worked in business. But now I know that the laws of business are in many ways the laws of life. And of vacations!'

8. Reach out and grab someone

You're never more alone than when you've just blown it. Your colleagues are busy making you the scapegoat. Your subordinates have just had their faith in you shaken. Your boss is on the phone to the headhunters. And everybody else is just staring at you in horror and fascination. It can get gruesome. Reach out! Call a friend or your spouse and tell them you need to talk. The benefits are that they will remind you (one would hope) that you're not the idiot you think you are, they can help you identify solutions, and finally, talking just feels good. Let down any facades you may have built up to convince others that you're invincible. Going at it alone is too much hard work.

9. Remove chronic mistake makers

It's necessary. If someone is habitually making a mistake and not learning from it or correcting it, you must take action. Mistakes cause bad information to get into your system, and once it's there it's very difficult to get out; it tends to rear its ugly head when you least expect it. Without the benefit of the lesson and the correction, mistakes just aren't worth the hassle. Look at it this way: People deserve the opportunity to be in a position where they can succeed. You're not doing anyone a favour by keeping someone in a position where he or she chronically makes mistakes. (But what if you're the chronic mistake maker? Then ask to be placed in a position that matches your skills.)

10. Never attempt a cover-up

When things go wrong, don't react, as so many do, by looking for ways to cover up. You made a mistake, it is probably obvious to everyone, and you are accountable for it. So admit it. It's tedious to deal with someone who refuses to acknowledge a mistake or becomes defensive over it.

One of the most important lessons professionals must learn is that they're obliged to fulfil their responsibilities, no matter what the mitigating circumstances are. In college you may have been able to get away with excuses like 'I didn't know we were going to be tested on those chapters', or 'My girlfriend left me and I'm a mess', or 'My dog ate my term paper'. (This last likely story was actually used by a fellow student in one of Jeff's political science classes — and accepted by the professor.) But in the real world, forgetting, misunderstanding, assuming, and being let down by other people (or animals) do not get you off the hook.

Being accountable for your own work is tough enough, but it gets really stressful when you become accountable for the work of the people you supervise. People — even the most trustworthy and competent people — sometimes make stupid mistakes, and it's impossible to predict them. Say, for example, you are at a client's office delivering a presentation, and you realize that your secretary has neglected to include the all-important budget figures. You told your secretary twice to be sure to include them, and clearly conveyed the importance of everything being right for this presentation. But now you are standing in front of your client, and it is perfectly clear that for one reason or another the budget figures are not to be found.

There are a couple of ways to handle this situation. The way *not* to handle it is to blame it on your secretary, as if denying direct responsibility absolves you. Your client doesn't care if your secretary is incompetent or had a bad day. The internal workings of your organization are your problem, and it's your responsibility to see that your organization does its job properly. All your client cares about is that you were supposed to bring the budget figures, and you did not bring them. Far better to say something like, 'Obviously we had a breakdown in preparing this presentation. I'll bring you the budget figures by the end of the day. I'm sorry.'

Another common excuse 'unprofessionals' use to escape their accountability is: 'There was nothing I could do about it'. Suppose, for example, you are responsible for getting an important package to an air courier service for delivery the next day. The deadline for getting the package to the courier is six o'clock. You arrive at five-thirty, only to find that the courier has changed its deadline to five o'clock. The plane your package had to be on left a half-hour ago. There's nothing you can do. You turn around and walk out.

You know everyone at your office is going to be terribly upset, so by the time you arrive there the next morning, with the unshipped package in your hands, you've rehearsed your story a thousand times in your head. 'I am so upset', you announce, eager to align yourself with everyone else. 'Air Courier changed their deadline schedule to five o'clock and didn't tell any of their customers about it. The deadline has always been six o'clock, and I go in there last night and suddenly they tell me they've moved it to five. How was I supposed to know?'

That may *sound* like a good enough excuse, but it falls short on many counts. First of all, as the person in charge of seeing that packages are delivered, you should have chosen a more dependable air courier, or developed a better relationship with this one so that they would have notified you of a scheduling change.

Second, you assumed that since the deadline had always been six o'clock it would always be six o'clock. That's assuming too much. Considering the importance of this package, you should have called the courier to double check, leaving nothing to chance.

Third, you accepted defeat far too easily. This was your biggest mistake. When Air Courier turned out to be an impossibility, you didn't check with other air courier companies. Worse yet, you didn't call your boss, thus precluding any opportunities he or she may have had to remedy the situation (like hand delivering the package via a commercial flight if it was important enough, or at least calling the recipient to minimize the damage). Instead, because you felt you were covered ('How was I to know?'), you either didn't think to try anything else or didn't want to bother. But a big part of being a professional is knowing when and how to ad-lib. Things rarely go exactly the way they are supposed to go. If you throw your hands up in defeat at the first problem you run into — even if it's due to unforeseen circumstances or someone else's mistake — you will never earn the 'can-do' reputation you need to be a respected and trusted member of your organization.

Your first reaction to a mistake should be to do what you can to put things back on course or minimize the damage. After that, look at the situation with an eye towards seeing what you could have done to avoid it altogether, and thereby ensure that you'll never do it again.

11. Show some remorse

Almost as bad as refusing to admit your mistake is refusing to admit it's done damage. Never trivialize a mistake or shrug it off with an 'Oh, well, everything will work out'. If people think you don't care about the mistakes you make, they will have no faith in your motivation to improve. There has to be an emotional catharsis. Your mistake *has* upset things; you must show it has upset *you*, too. You don't have to throw yourself on the floor and wail, but it might not be a bad idea to approach your boss and say something like, 'I know I really messed things up, and I want you to know I'm sorry.'

Now, what if your mistake wasn't exactly an honest one, but actually the result of negligence or insubordination? Even in embarrassing cases like these, accountability is the best policy. For instance, you might say to your boss, 'I know I was supposed to get the bids in writing, but I was under pressure and thought I could let it slide this one time. It's caused a lot of problems, I know. I'm really sorry. It won't happen again.'

12. Demonstrate the lesson

Make sure the people around you know you have turned your mistake into a good lesson. The best way to do this is to systematize the process, with a 'One Mistake I'll Never Make Again' sheet (see Figure 13.1). As we've said, the process of writing an idea imprints it on your mind. When you've completed this sheet, send it out as a memo to affected parties (like your boss) and then file a copy. It pays to enforce this system among your staff, too; just make sure you do it in the spirit of growth, not punishment. You may all want to get together with your files occasionally to remind yourselves, as the saying at the bottom of the form suggests, how much cleverer you are than you used to be.

ONE MISTAKE I'LL NEVER MAKE AGAIN

1. What the mistake was (describe actual events):

2. Why it happened (I forgot, someone let me down, I didn't follow the system, etc.):

3. What I did to fix it or minimize the damage (what's salvageable, what's the opportunity?):

4. What I did so it will never happen again (set up file, get educated, changed the system, etc.):

5. Other mistakes-in-waiting I can fix, or opportunities I can take advantage of because of this lesson:

Isn't it great to be so much cleverer?

Figure 13.1   'One Mistake I'll Never Make Again' sheet

Delegate Work and Make Sure It's Done Right

You Can't Do It All by Yourself

*If something is worth doing, it is worth
telling someone else how to do it well.*
    — FRANKLIN P. JONES,
    THE WALL STREET JOURNAL

No matter how productive you think you are, at some
point you will reach your limit. To go beyond this limit
of what is humanly possible for one person to accomplish,
you have to get other people to share and support your
goal. Whether you supervise one person or command a
multinational conglomerate, you must be able to effectively delegate work if you want to move up — and stay
up.

Improving your delegation skills will free you to take
on higher challenges. By developing the people who work
under you, you will be grooming your successor. Generally, not until you've trained your replacement can you
move to higher ground. As you pass on power, you create
more for yourself.

Another benefit of delegating effectively is that you
accomplish more. With an expanded sphere of control and
productivity, you can leverage more goals in the same
amount of time.

Delegating work is one thing; making sure it's done
right is another. Remember, no matter how good you become at delegating, you can never delegate the ultimate
responsibility for the work your people do. Managers often
delegate and then are disappointed with what comes back
— it's either wrong or late. So a big part of good delegation
is *monitoring* the project — in other words, striking the
right balance between delegating and forgetting about it,
and pulling all the strings from behind the scenes.

Knowing how to delegate is obviously a critical management and leadership skill. It is often the key difference

between managers who exceed their limit because they can't let go and those whose upward mobility is unlimited. Learn it.

THE HOW-TO-DO-ITS

1. Develop a 'delegation consciousness'

The obvious first step in deciding what you can delegate is to make sure you're clear on exactly what it is that you do (don't laugh, many professionals really couldn't tell you all the tasks they do day after day). For the next couple of days, stop before each task and consider it for a moment. Is it something only you can do? Is it something you want to continue doing? Could it be delegated? To whom, and under what circumstances?

Generally you'll identify for delegation the jobs that have become routine and unchallenging to you. By delegating them you keep yourself growing. You also keep your people growing. Just because you're bored with a task doesn't mean it couldn't be a wonderful challenge for someone else (just remember to delegate the fun jobs, too). Ask yourself, 'What decisions do I make more often? Where do my subordinates need development? Which tasks am I ready to let go of?' Also, ask your subordinates what they think you should pass on — maybe they're better qualified than you to judge. Figure 14.1 shows a chart that will help you sort out what you do and which things you can delegate.

2. Clarify the task in your own mind

One of the most common office complaints is 'I don't know what I'm supposed to be doing'. You can solve this problem, as the boss, by making sure *you* know what it is you want your employees to do. You can clarify any project for them by asking yourself a couple of questions: 'How will I know when it's done? How will it look?' Before you delegate anything, make sure the result is specific and measurable in your own mind. Then delegate it that way. (Instead of saying, 'Contact

WHAT TO DELEGATE

	What I do	What I would like to delegate	Who could do it now	Who could do it with training	What type of training
1.					
2.					
3.					
4.					
5.					
6.					

Figure 14.1   What to delegate

every customer', try 'Send every customer a catalogue and cover letter by Friday'.

3. Pick the right people

It's essential that you present subordinates with challenges that fit their next level of growth. If you underchallenge a person, he or she will quickly get bored and leave. If you overchallenge, you'll have a very frustrated and unhappy employee. Mastering this is more an art than a science, but there is one easy way of improving your accuracy — look at the people who have expressed an interest. Who's been on at you for more of a challenge? Who's dying to have a shot at a job like this? Open your mind even to people who may not seem to be qualified — often an ounce of enthusiasm is worth a pound of experience. This kind of creative delegation also sends a positive message to your organization: people can create their own opportunities and make their own paths.

4. Delegate the result, not the process

In other words, make sure people see how the task relates to the 'big picture'. For instance, let's say you want to delegate to your assistant the responsibility for answering customer complaint letters. One way you could do this is to provide him with a few standard letters for different situations, so all he would have to do is insert the name and address. And you could prepare a checklist so he would always be certain to enclose the correct literature, alert the correct departments of the action taken, etc. The result? Your assistant gets another mindless job to do, and your customers get yet another standard letter.

There's a much better way. Delegate to your assistant the responsibility for seeing that complaining customers are satisfied. Start by showing him the importance to your business of good customer relations; explain that repeat business and word-of-mouth advertising are the backbone of your marketing effort. Tell him the story of how turning around just one customer resulted in more than $10000 in additional sales over the following year. Remind him that beyond the financial aspects, treating customers like real people is the best way and is a major tenet on which your company was built. Take the time to give him the details, colour, and drama.

Now you have somebody who is excited and proud of the job he's been delegated. And the truth of the matter is that the substance of the delegated task doesn't have to be all that different. It's still a good idea to give your assistant your standard letters and checklists. But now you encourage him (and empower him with the tools, time, and authority) to use his judgement. He may write a special letter to a customer with an unusual situation. Or call. Or send the letter with a case of free products if he judges the complaint to be extreme enough. You can always be there on the sidelines, helping him with his judgement, by pulling him back if he goes too far, cheering him on when he makes the right moves, and most of all letting him fail, learn, and succeed. If you do this skilfully (it's not hard, it just takes faith) you will have such a turned-on, productive, and effective employee you may not recognize him. And, incidentally, the outcome of his work (in this case the loyalty of your customers when they realize your company really does care) will pay for any added costs at least a hundred times over.

The point is that people don't take pride in processing letters, but they do take pride in being good with irate customers. Don't deprive them of this opportunity.

5. Don't overwhelm the delegate

Be careful not to overload your people with instructions and information. Remember, you know how to do it, but they don't — not yet, anyway. Give them just enough data to keep the process simple, yet ensure they know exactly what you want them to do. Resist the temptation to show off your knowledge or have a one-person public brainstorm about it. Irrelevant or esoteric facts that may be interesting to you will only confuse a novice.

6. Specify the level of authority

This is a key, yet often ignored, aspect of delegation. When you make people responsible, let them know how much authority they have to complete a project. Here's an example of three levels of authority: 1 'Look into the problem, give me your three best solutions, and I'll choose one'; 2 'Look into the problem, tell me how you plan to solve it, and do so unless I say otherwise'; 3 'Handle the problem and let me know what you did'. Tell them *exactly* how far they can go. When you delegate sufficient authority, you get commitment — and results — in return.

7. Recognize teaching moments

A classic example of a teaching moment is when your ten-year-old child asks, 'Mum and Dad, how are babies made?' At that moment you drop whatever you're doing and turn your attention to a child who is ready to learn something he or she needs to know. The same phenomenon happens in delegation. When your people come to you with an insightful question or opinion, they are extremely open to expanding their horizons and learning new skills. This is when the teaching moment turns into the delegation moment. In this sense, training and delegation are two sides of the same coin. By developing a sensitivity to teaching moments, you will become a far more effective delegator — and leader.

8. Let go

Once you've delegated a task, let your delegates have an honest, fair try at it. Don't meddle! Let them do it their way, even if it's not 'the right way' (their way *is* often better). If you take back or short-circuit assignments, your interfering will only frustrate your subordinates. Jimmy has a favourite quote he reminds himself of whenever he's about to delegate a cherished responsibility: 'When I let go, you grow'. Don't be afraid that what you delegate will be done better than you could have done it — if you pick the right person, it will be.

9. Resist 'upward delegation'

Upward delegation happens when one of your people with a new assignment comes in to your office to ask a question about it, and you say, 'Good question. I'll find out and let you know.' Now who's got the project? You do — it's been delegated back to you. How much better it would have been to tell the person how to find the answer (that would be valuable training) or even to say, 'You can figure it out — keep trying'. It not only saves you time but forces the person to break through his or her mental blocks. Just be careful not to show impatience or anger — send him or her back to the drawing board with a smile and a wink.

10. Monitor delegated tasks

Never forget: What you were responsible for before delegating, you are responsible for *after* delegating. To avoid letting a delegated task get away from you, set up automatic system checks so you'll get regular 'flash reports' (weekly, daily, or monthly — whatever is appropriate) on how it's coming along. As a result of these reports you may be able to readjust the project based on new data. Or you may find the project in chaos, at which time you can get involved. The best way to get a surprise in business is to delegate a project and forget about it till it's due. And in business, surprises are rarely good.

11. Don't penalize fumbles

Just make sure you and your delegates learn from them (see Success Shortcut 13). As American manufacturer Arthur Jones put it, 'Success comes from good judgment. Good judgment comes from experience. Experience comes from bad judgment.' If the consequences aren't too great, watch your people do it wrong the first time, so they'll appreciate the right way next time. When you punish learning behaviour you paralyse the members of your staff and undermine their confidence. If they fear reprimands and criticism, they'll take fewer risks and ultimately perform poorly. One way to minimize mistakes is to have your instructions repeated back to you. Take an extra minute to make sure you've communicated precisely and to clarify what's not 100 per cent clear. Doing this will save you from having to hear, 'Yes, but I thought you said...'

12. Acknowledge your 'occupational hobbies'

These are the duties you should have delegated a long time ago, but haven't because they're too much fun. It's OK to keep a couple (as in two, not ten), but at least recognize them for what they are: easy, enjoyable, and much better done by somebody else. Oh, well, what's the use of reaching your goals if you can't enjoy it?

Write Easily and Be Understood

You're as Good as Your Words

The discipline of writing something down is the first step toward making it happen.
— LEE IACOCCA

The most important benefit of powerful writing is that it enables you to make yourself understood. That's no small feat. The professional world is plagued with all sorts of misread instructions, confused agreements, and crossed signals due to poor writing. By presenting your ideas clearly in writing and keeping track of important information, you minimize this kind of commotion in your professional life.

Another advantage of powerful writing is that when you present complex ideas in a way people can easily understand, you are regarded as being more intelligent, maybe even brilliant. Powerful writing impresses people, opens doors, and creates opportunities. That's as it should be. By forcing you to think through and organize what you have to say, good writing does make you 'cleverer'.

Writing is also a proven leadership skill. If you can get to the level in your writing where you can communicate your personality and feelings, you will be able to touch people on an emotional as well as an intellectual level. This is a great way to motivate people.

Clearly, developing powerful writing skills is well worth the trouble. And, unfortunately, it *takes* a little trouble. Even though writing is a fundamental skill which we have been practising nearly all our lives, getting *really good* at it can be gruelling, frustrating work.

In written as in spoken communications, we deal in two commodities: facts and feelings. Business writing deals, for the most part, in facts. The primary purpose of a memo, report, contract, instruction, or evaluation is to communicate or record data. But even though feelings play the smaller role in this kind of writing, they are not to be ignored. It is a rare memo or report that can't be made more effective by conveying a little personality or point of view.

So ultimately facts and feelings are rarely used exclusively of each other in writing. The trick is to know how, when, and to what degree to combine the two.

Facts-oriented business writing is relatively easy, which makes one wonder why so many people do it so badly. When dealing with facts, all you have to do is ask yourself, 'What do I want to say?' Write it down. Then ask yourself, 'Now what do I want to say?' And write *it* down. Continue this process, keeping it relaxed and random, until you have said it all. Then go back and put it in order. Find the big ideas and support them with the small ideas. Add and delete as you see fit.

Once you have supported and ordered your ideas logically, commit them to paper as clearly and objectively as you can. Pretend you are *Star Trek's* Mr Spock. Lead your reader by the hand; leave nothing open to misunderstanding. For example:

> Our 1987 sales volume in Europe was down 19 per cent from 1986. There are three reasons for the decline. First, Europe's domestic industries are catching up with our technology. In England, for instance . . .

This is simple writing, but good writing. And if it is as far as you advance, you will still be well ahead of most people.

To become a really powerful communicator, of course, you will have to add feeling to your writing. This is where you can run into trouble. In spoken communication, feelings are expressed through tone of voice and body language, as well as through word choice. In writing, all we have is the last. Also, since feelings are, by necessity, subjective and intangible, it is difficult to be sure your reader receives the message you think you are sending. For instance, when describing an ingot of steel in terms of its dimensions, weight, and chemical specifications, you can be pretty sure your reader will be able to create a mental image close to what you intend. But if you try to write about the sensual aspect of touching steel, or of watching steel being made, it is impossible to create a precise mental picture. So *forget* about communicating a precise mental picture. Make it your goal to provide a framework upon which the reader can create his or her own mental picture. The reader's resulting personalized image will be much more powerful.

Treat feelings in your writing in much the same way as you treat facts: clearly and directly. And sparingly. For example:

> I believe it would be a mistake for us to continue directing our resources toward re-establishing dominance in the European market. It's time we cut our losses. This may be difficult to swallow after all the work we have done, but it is a fact we must face.

Injecting a little feeling and personality into your writing can spice it nicely. But be careful. In writing, as in cooking, while a little spice is nice, a lot is rarely better. Don't let emotion overpower your message.

THE HOW-TO-DO-ITS

1. Know *when* to write

Written communication is often far more powerful than spoken communication. This is particularly true if you have not yet developed a 'silver tongue'. For instance, if you have an important idea to sell to your boss or team, try presenting it in written form. It will immediately take on more importance, and you won't have to worry about getting flustered or forgetting a key point. Writing also adds power when you're making a request, dealing with a conflict, giving praise or gratitude, cementing agreements . . . in virtually all communications.

2. Write it all before you rewrite any of it

Sit down, keep forging ahead, don't correct, and don't regress. When you've the raw material down you can go back and put it in better order, rewrite sentences, and add the supporting points and transitions that make good writing. Much of your first draft will not be usable, but you may be surprised at how good some of it is. A trick is to force yourself to plough through the first two or three sentences, even if they make no sense. In fact, *expect* that they will make no sense. They're the necessary warm-ups. Writers often get bogged down simply because they won't let go of a sentence until it is perfect.

3. Make your point in the beginning

Don't force your reader to wade through your writing to get your main point. Use the classic newswriting formula, the 'inverted pyramid'. Make your most important point first, your second-most important point next, and so on. What this formula lacks in creativity, it more than makes up for in accuracy and clarity. And besides, if you're worried about all your business writing being 'creative', you're not going to get anything else done.

4. Start with a 'greased chute'

The most difficult part of writing is getting started. The same is true of reading. So do yourself *and* your reader a favour by making your first sentence short and simple. This is an advertising technique, called the 'greased chute' (developed by the legendary American copywriter Joe Sugarman), that is also effective in business writing. Your first sentence doesn't even have to be a sentence. It could be a fragment, a single word, a quote, even a cliché. Here are some good examples of the short, engaging first sentence: 'Picture this'. 'It's time to make a change'. 'Let's be blunt'.

Of course, for every example supporting the concept of the short opening sentence, there is an example from literature which blows it apart. One of the most striking of the latter is the opening sentence of Scott Spencer's novel, *Endless Love:* 'When I was seventeen and in full obedience to my heart's most urgent commands, I stepped far from the pathway of normal life and in a moment's time ruined everything I loved — I loved so deeply, and when the love was in terror and my own body was locked away, it was hard for others to believe that a life so new could suffer so irrevocably.' It's hard *not* to continue reading after that. (Caution: This kind of writing is best left for novelists.)

5. Use subheads (and graphics)

Subheads serve two valuable functions. First, they break up long bodies of writing, thus making them less intimidating and easier to understand. Second, they index ideas so the reader can locate sections of special interest. If you have access to computers and word processors with graphics capabilities, you can add even more appeal and organization to your writing by spicing it with various typefaces and symbols.

6. Be stingy with words

Don't waste people's time by overexplaining. It's a typical writer's mistake to want to say everything there is to say about a subject. A good rule of thumb (enforced ruthlessly at the highest levels of many businesses) is: 'If you can't say it on one side of a sheet of paper, you haven't thought it out enough'. In writing, less *is* more.

7. Break the rules

Of course, before you break the rules it's a good idea to learn them — at least the basic ones. But ultimately the purpose of writing is to communicate. As long as your writing is clear and accurate, don't worry about the strict rules of grammar. Sentence fragments, creative punctuation, made-up-at-the-spur-of-the-moment compound adjectives (like that one) all add sparkle and life to the written word. There are two exceptions to this. One is when you know you're writing for a strict grammarian. In that case, you just might want to humour him or her. The second regards spelling: there's nothing creative about a misspelt word.

8. Vary the lengths of your sentences

Don't use only short sentences. Or long ones. Especially one after the other. That can be very annoying. See what we mean? Give your writing a good, comfortable rhythm by varying the lengths of your sentences. To get a feel for the rhythm in your writing, try reading it aloud.

9. 'Thesaurus-ize' it

When only the right word will do, a thesaurus is invaluable. Keep one nearby and consult it often. It not only will improve the quality of your writing but also will build your vocabulary. (The difference between a poor vocabulary and a great one is only about 2500 words.) Also, did you know that *thesaurus* means 'treasure house'? It's a nice thought.

10. Close with a BANG!

Don't just stop writing. Summarize your points, ask for action, state a moral, and tell them what you told them. The best way to make sure your readers are clear about your message is to leave it ringing in their ears. Incidentally, it's been shown that the most remembered part of a letter is the P.S. — that's why direct-mail advertising letters almost always have a P.S. You can use it in your letters, too, to re-emphasize your main point or request. 'P.S. Just before he died he wrote you back into his will.' Wouldn't this postscript make you want to go back to the beginning of the letter and read it word for word?

11. Sleep on it

As Mario Puzo, author of *The Godfather*, says, 'It's all in the rewrite'. Don't burden yourself with striving to write the perfect first draft, particularly with important documents. Take advantage of the power of the second or third draft. And let some time elapse. You'll be amazed at the perspective a night's sleep can give your writing. Your points will come together more coherently, your transitions will tighten, and you'll have no trouble coming up with the perfect word that eluded you in earlier drafts.

12. Get a second opinion

And a third or fourth, for that matter. This is insurance against writing something really stupid (writers are known for *completely* losing perspective on their own writing). It's also an opportunity for someone to suggest a new way to organize your material, to clarify a cloudy point, or to suggest a killer turn of phrase. If you have a secretary or typist, encourage him or her to fix your mistakes and suggest ways to improve your writing. Find a 'Maxwell Perkins' (the celebrated editor for F. Scott Fitzgerald and Ernest Hemingway) whom you can trust to give you good advice. You might even consider teaming up with an associate and developing a writing partnership for your most important business letters and reports.

The tips we've just presented will help you improve your writing the first time you try them. But the only way to become a truly powerful writer is to write. Like all skills, writing gets better with practice. Make strengthening your writing ability a priority in your professional development. You'll appreciate the results.

Sell Yourself and Your Ideas

The Anatomy of Influence

No army can withstand the strength of
an idea whose time has come.
— VICTOR HUGO

Ideas are the raw material of success. The better you are at selling your ideas and getting the support of others, the faster and further you'll go.

But still — sell yourself? Sell your ideas? Sounds a little pushy, doesn't it? After all, an idea should stand on its own. Well, maybe it should, but often it doesn't. In fact, 'an idea whose time has come' may be ignored, if not actively resisted. An update of Victor Hugo's famous line shown above would be 'No army can withstand the strength of an idea whose time has come, in the hands of someone who can sell it'.

Persuasiveness is a hard-to-pin-down quality that is made up of a number of ingredients: commitment, eloquence, honesty, enthusiasm, and humour. But no matter how difficult it is to define, it is *essential* to develop.

The ability to sell yourself and your ideas is a key element of charisma. Persuasive people always first sell themselves, because they know that people do business with people they like and trust. In that way persuasiveness increases your professional profile.

Whatever your motivation for becoming more persuasive, you have your work cut out for you. Getting people to accept your new ideas may require that they change their habits or general view — and that takes a lot of effort. Also, people can be jealous about new ideas. A good idea represents value and power, and your associates may resent the fact that you had the idea and they don't (and now you expect them to embrace it?).

So it turns out that everybody is in sales. Whether your title is sales representative or accounting manager, you sell for a living. Whether you're negotiating a multinational deal, persuading your marketing department to take on a new product, selling a copy machine, asking for the afternoon off, or convincing your spouse to go out to dinner, you sell for a living. Your success, then, depends not only on the merit of the product, but also on your powers of persuasion.

THE HOW-TO-DO-ITS

1. Know what you want, exactly

Your chances of selling an idea rise in proportion to how well you have clarified the idea in your own mind. Don't go into a negotiation or persuasion situation with the goal of getting the best deal or 'as much as you can get'. Instead, specify *on paper* your exact goal, with numbers, key players, deadlines, and budgets. This doesn't mean you should be inflexible in the process of selling an idea. It's simply that the clearer and more committed you are at the outset, the stronger you are as a persuader.

2. Plan 'B' and 'C'

Develop a series of fall-back positions. This ensures that if your first idea is defeated you are not left with nothing. Rather, you have a 'Plan B' and 'Plan C' that you can instantly revert to and sell. Again, don't let planning inhibit flexibility — use it to give you strength.

3. Send up a trial balloon

Before you try to sell an idea, particularly a big or risky idea, it usually pays to assess the opposition. That's the purpose of a trial balloon. Trial ballooning means presenting your idea as a question or speculation. Instead of saying, 'Here's what I think we should do', say, 'I wonder what would happen if we...' The advantage of trial ballooning is that you separate yourself from your idea. That way, if it's shot down, you're not shot down with it. Knowing the extent of your opposition will tell you how to prepare the sales effort, how to modify your idea, whether you should abandon it, or if it's a likely winner.

4. Make your idea their idea

The one thing harder than getting people to buy your idea is getting them to give you credit for it. Therefore, one good way to get support is to give away the credit and ownership. By skilfully making suggestions and floating trial balloons, you can often get people to adopt your ideas as their own. One of the great old sayings of business is, 'It's amazing how much you can accomplish if you don't mind who gets the credit'.

Back when Jeff was starting in the advertising business, he had a client whose company made camping equipment (tents, sleeping bags, stoves, etc.) and sold it by mail. The client, Mr. Baxter, decided to include in his catalogue a new line of camping clothing, such as windpants, nylon socks, and windbreakers. He asked Jeff, as his advertising copywriter, to come to the meeting where this idea would be presented to the marketing department. Mr. Baxter owned the company 100 per cent — he could do anything he wanted — so, naturally, Jeff expected a typical presentation from 'the boss'. What Jeff actually saw was one of the most beautiful professional performances he'd ever witnessed.

Mr. Baxter started the meeting with business as usual, nothing new. About a half-hour into the meeting, he leaned back in his chair, took a deep breath, and said, 'Gee, I wonder what would happen if we added this new line of clothing to our catalogue?'

Everybody, of course, had a natural resistance to this idea. The man from shipping and receiving said, 'Clothing? It's a nightmare selling clothing! It doesn't fit; people return it. You don't know the problems selling clothing. You think we have problems with returns now, you wait.'

The woman from the art department said, 'And you know what else? We'd have to hire models, we'd have to join the union, we'd have to deal with prima donnas, we'd have to hire better photographers. It would be a nightmare selling clothing.'

And the person from the letter shop, who did the mailings, said, 'And we'd have to add pages to the catalogue. It would be heavier, postage would go up — and you know how expensive postage is. A nightmare.'

Mr. Baxter listened, because, truly, they were good, legitimate concerns. In fact, he agreed with these objections and helped guide his employees to their own solutions with trial balloon statements such as, 'I wonder if we could ...' and 'what do you think about ...' and 'it might be possible to ...' Then, after the orgy of negativity had died down, he came back with a statement that turned the tide: 'You know, those are all good reasons why this wouldn't work. Now let's think of some reasons why it would.' People will play along with this kind of suggestion, and the people at the meeting did.

The man from shipping and receiving said, 'You know, our competitors are selling clothing by mail. They found a way to make it work; I guess we can, too, since we're better than they are.'

The woman from the art department said, 'Models are a problem, but the fact is that sportswear has become a multi-billion-dollar industry in this country. People wear $200 tennis shoes — I guess they probably want to look good in the wilderness, too.'

The man from the letter shop said, 'And, you know, I have another idea for all of you. We should be selling freezedried food.' Another person suggested, 'We should add a middle section to our catalogue where people can buy and sell their used equipment.' (This classified advertising section, by the way, has turned out to be one of the most profitable parts of their catalogue.) Unrelated ideas like these can come forth when you create a climate of 'let's think of reasons why things will work'.

The best part of this story, though, is that by the end of the meeting Mr. Baxter's idea really was their idea. They had found holes in Mr. Baxter's plan and fixed them. After all, these were the people on the front lines, the people who were dealing with problems that Mr. Baxter hadn't dealt with in years, so they really did improve his idea.

What Mr. Baxter didn't get was the ego boost of everybody standing around after the meeting saying, 'Boy, what a great idea Mr. Baxter had!' But you know what? They weren't going to say that anyway; that's not how people operate. Knowing this, Mr. Baxter was more than willing to get co-operation by giving away the credit.

Making your idea their idea works best when you are in a position of authority, because it increases your people's ownership of and commitment to an idea. When you're not in the boss's role, however, you may not want to give away credit. After all, getting recognized for your ideas is a major way of moving ahead in an organization. If you find yourself in a situation where you could lose the credit, you may decide to follow up selling your idea with a memo outlining the action steps and thanking people for their support. That way you clarify ownership without coming across as greedy and territorial.

5. Phrase it in terms of their interests

This is the oldest rule of salesmanship in the book, and for good reason: it works like a charm. People are far more likely to do something if it's clear how they will benefit. If you want your marketing team to adopt a risky new product, show them how they'll all be heroes if it works. Paint the benefit in the most appealing and colourful terms possible. Before presenting an idea, take the time to write across the top of a sheet of paper, 'What's in it for them?' Then keep that benefit foremost in your mind — and theirs — throughout your presentation.

6. Ask for more than you want

If you're really committed to your idea, you can probably stretch your commitment to include a few extra goodies. It's rare that an idea is accepted and implemented without some negotiation. So make sure you build concession room into your deadlines, budgets, and other critical areas. If you sell your idea particularly skilfully and end up getting more than you need, you can put yourself in the wonderful position of coming in under budget or ahead of deadline. Your next idea will be that much easier to sell.

7. Get a 'yes' early on

A good first impression is just as important for an idea as it is for a person. Therefore, it usually pays to start a negotiation on a point with which your audience can agree. It can be a minor point, even irrelevant. A copy machine sales rep we know starts his presentation by asking the buyer, 'Ms. Smith, before I explain our product, I would like to ask you some questions about your copier usage. Is that all right?' Of course her answer is yes. And the positive frame of mind — the 'yes patter' — has been established. Try it, it works.

8. Get a 'no' early on

It's been said that a characteristic of a mature mind is the ability to hold two diametrically opposed ideas at the same time. Reconciling points seven and eight is your opportunity to practise. If you sense the people in your audience are insecure about their power (and therefore need to assert it) or jealous of your idea, let them say no about something minor early on. Throw them a bone. Once they've demonstrated their power to disagree, they are usually more open to agree.

9. Anchor it in writing

Writing adds weight to an idea. This tactic works beautifully if you are trying to sell to a very busy person and having a hard time getting his or her attention. People like this usually know that most ideas are half-baked in both concept and commitment. They trust that, if it's important enough, you'll get their attention. Writing is a good way to do just that. It's also a good technique if you aren't yet confident of your verbal presentation skills. (Sales tip: keep your idea to one page and mention only the best points. Also, ask for a response within a specific amount of time; that's a good way to produce a response. Another way to add pressure is to send photocopies to other significant parties, such as the boss.)

10. Answer objections with benefits

Inevitably people will come up with reasons why your ideas won't work. Accept and respect both the objections and the objectors. Don't make it your goal to overcome their objections by showing them the error of their logic or philosophy. Just come back by reiterating what's in it for them.

One of Jeff's favourite salespeople is a woman named Susan who works in a clothing store at which Jeff regularly shops. A while back, he was planning a speaking tour of Australia and needed a new suit for the occasion. When he walked into the store, Susan greeted him, saying, 'Jeff, I'm really happy to see you. It's great that you came in now because we just happen to have a brand new Giorgio Armani suit in your size. It's going to be beautiful on you.'

Jeff tried on the suit in front of a mirror, and while he was admiring his reflection he casually asked Susan how much the suit cost. She said: 'Eight hundred dollars.'

Jeff was deflated. He said, 'Susan, you know I would never spend $800 on a suit.'

Her response was short and confident. She said simply, 'Look at yourself in that suit. You look fabulous.' She didn't argue with him about how much he ought to spend. She didn't tell him that lots of people spend that much on a suit. She didn't suggest that somebody going all the way to Australia to speak before thousands of people ought to wear an $800 suit. She made no mention of the store's wonderful credit policy or free tailoring or anything else.

Jeff said, 'Susan, $800 for two pieces of material!?'

Susan replied, 'Imagine walking into a seminar wearing that suit.' She didn't engage in any of his arguments; she just kept complimenting him. (By the way, Jeff really loves his new suit!)

A good rule of thumb when you're answering objections with benefits, and one that Susan knows perfectly, is 'When you're blue in the face, they're just beginning to get it'. Don't assume that people heard you the first time. Also, consider raising and resolving the potential objections yourself, before your opponents do. That way you preempt their element of surprise, and prove you have nothing to hide.

11. Go higher

If you have a boss who obstructs your good ideas, consider going over his or her head. It's risky, but it might pay off. At first, invite your boss along: 'I know you think this is a terrible idea, but I'm still really excited about it. I'd like to suggest that we both go to Mr. Martin to see what he thinks.' Often the mere 'threat' will get your boss moving. If he or she declines your invitation, advise him or her that you are going alone. Then do it. As we said, this is risky and you could lose your job (although our research shows this rarely happens). But if you're really committed to your ideas, what's the alternative?

12. Show your gratitude

Few actions have a better cost/benefit ratio than a thank-you note. Whether you've negotiated a major deal, made a sale, or got Friday afternoon off, take the time to show your appreciation. It eliminates any bad feelings that might be left over from a tough negotiation, and sets the mode for a good implementation. It also overcomes 'buyer's remorse', that 'what-have-I-done?' feeling that often accompanies a purchase. Plus it feels so good that people are more inclined to support you in the future. Your thank-you will be a hundred times more powerful if it's put in writing. In most cases, a two- or three-sentence handwritten note will do. 'Thanks for the green light. I can't wait to get started. You won't be sorry!' That's all you need to say.

Make Presentations That Win Support

Talk Ain't Cheap

Standing ovation or polite applause?
— BERN WHEELER

Public speaking is a Class A success skill. No skill opens more doors, creates more visibility, or gives you more opportunity to exercise power. Right or wrong, fair or unfair, the person who's capable of articulating an idea is usually credited with having had it. When you're a good presenter, you're seen as an idea person (and you are one). Also, when you've educated people, sparked ideas, and opened minds, you remind yourself of how much you know and how good you are.

Presentations are terrific opportunities to convert listeners into buyers and doers. In a public speaking situation you're not talking off the cuff (in most cases); you have time to prepare your points. You can present your argument at your own speed, with no interruptions, holding your audience's complete attention. When it comes to changing minds and swaying opinions, one knock-'em-dead presentation is worth three arguments at a meeting, ten memos, and fifty one-on-one pleas.

And, holding an audience's attention feels *great*. Most people have had stage or playing-field fantasies of being the centre of attention. Public speaking is the business equivalent, an acceptable and profitable way of exercising your 'performance' tendencies.

If you have the talent and discipline to become a pro at public speaking, you'll find that you have developed a strong leadership skill. Whether it's the warmth and intimacy or the fire and brimstone approach, people respond to good oratory as they respond to nothing else.

Think about how strong presentation skills can help you, while making a sales call, presenting your department's latest accomplishments at your weekly meeting, explaining a new system to management, kicking off an important meeting or discussion group, teaching a seminar at an industry convention. The opportunities are plentiful. Here's how you can capitalize on them.

THE HOW-TO-DO-ITS

1. Create opportunities to speak

Presentations are too valuable in your career for you to leave them to chance. Think about what you know that would be of value to other people. Has your department come up with a new system, product, or solution that your upper management or other departments ought to know about? Offer to make a presentation! Also, what do you know about that would be of interest to the scores of civic organizations in your community, or even to your professional associations? Some groups pay speakers a token fee, but even if you speak for free, the experience and exposure are well worth the effort.

2. Tell a story

And use it to make a point. Remember when you were a kid sitting around the campfire listening to ghost stories? You were enthralled and terrified, hanging on every word. It's no different in business: tell a story and you'll have them on the edge of their seats. Stories are your way of bringing to life the points you are making. People love the colour and drama of a good story, and while they may forget some of the details of your point, they will integrate its substance via the story. In fact, if you want to capture an audience's attention immediately, just begin with, 'Hello, my name is _____ and I want to tell you a story'.

3. Repeat the important points over and over

You might feel like a kindergarten teacher, but you *will* get your points across. We remember seeing a motivational sales speaker, Alan Cimberg, who summarized his key points every time he made a new one, about every five minutes. In fact, he would command the audience to recite his key points back to him, almost like at a sing-along. Although it seemed corny and contrived at first, we ended up enjoying it and did remember his points (and still do). Keep 'telling them what you're telling them' and you'll get your message across.

4. Let them take a look

Some people can absorb information more easily visually than auditorially. A picture is still worth a thousand words, and some things that can't be described easily in words, such as sales projections or other data, can be communicated instantaneously with pictures or charts. This is particularly true today, since people are accustomed to getting information through the visual media of television, magazines, and even newspapers. There are many ways to create good presentation visuals. New technology such as lettering machines and personal computers can generate graphs, charts, headlines, and pictograms. You can even photocopy your information on acetate for overhead projection.

5. Rehearse your lines

Don't expect them just to 'come to you' while you're on stage — trust us, they won't. Yet you want to make it seem that way to the audience. That takes practice (ever noticed how a joke gets funnier each time you tell it?). The only way to practise speaking is to *start talking* — to a mirror, a wall, thin air, your kids, dogs, or stuffed animals. Don't get bogged down in organizing and reorganizing your material (that's not practising your speech; that's called practising *avoidance*). The fact is, rehearsing your delivery is one of the best ways to actually write, organize, and polish a speech. When you're hearing it you have a much better feel for what is working and what belongs where.

From time to time as a professional you are going to run into situations where you absolutely have to come across as a cool customer: when you ask for a salary, go into a job interview, or *make an important presentation*, for instance. Never leave these situations to chance. Never just assume you will say the right things. Even when you know, without a doubt, what you want to say, knowing it and saying it remain two different matters, especially when under pressure.

So say it beforehand. The best way to prepare for the really special performances of your professional life is to practise your lines until you know them by heart. Start by writing them down. Mentally put yourself in the situation you are about to face. If you are going to ask for a rise, for instance, imagine yourself sitting across from your boss. What are some of the ways you could begin your request? What are his or her possible responses? What are your possible responses to his or her possible responses? Be specific. There are hundreds of variables, of course, but as you imagine the situation you will begin to get a feeling for the major issues, and the best ways to address them.

The next step is actually to write a script for your major speeches. In asking for a rise the speech might consist of: 1   the opening monologue (breaking the ice and stating the request); 2   how much you want and the three or four major reasons you deserve it (your added responsibilities, seniority, the new business you have generated for the company, etc.); 3   your rebuttals to your boss's likely objections ('There's no money in the budget'); and, very important, 4   what you will say if ultimately you do not get what you want (Will you settle for another salary review in six months? Will you resign?). You might also create a couple of optional monologues to use if the situation warrants (for instance, the things you like about your job, or where you see yourself going in the company).

It is important to practise these speeches *out loud*. Don't just write them down and read them; that just gives you the illusion of knowing them. Actually recite them, even if it's just to the wall.

Obviously, it's impossible to plan for *every* contingency, so don't even try. Besides, it's better to stay a little flexible. If you have a strict scenario in mind when you enter a big role, you will become hopelessly lost the first time events violate your assumptions. The goal of rehearsing is to be able to go into a performance certain you have a clear, defensible position on the major issues, and knowing that you can deliver it clearly and confidently.

6. Manage the jitters

Nervousness before a presentation is inevitable — even good. As TV presenter Walter Cronkite says, 'It's natural to have butterflies. The secret is to get them to fly in formation.' When nervousness turns to dry mouth and heart palpitations, however, it can be a real problem. Here are a few suggestions on how to avoid debilitating nervousness: 1   know your material cold, and make sure your notes are clear and in order; 2   take a few deep breaths before you go on; 3   repeat affirmations to yourself (see Success Shortcut 1); and 4   visualize the audience sitting in their underwear. That's not entirely a joke; it can be quite calming to remind yourself that 'they're just people', and they're on your side.

7. Sell your message

This one point alone can bring a dead presentation to life. Don't just recite your information; tell your listeners how it will help them solve a problem or get what they want (features versus benefits, remember?). Tell them what you're about to tell them, and make a big promise in the process. To determine the most powerful what's-in-it-for-them promise, ask yourself, 'What's keeping them up at night?' If you're talking on stress management, for instance, introduce a point by saying, 'Now I'll show you how to pull yourself out of a bad mood in fifteen minutes', or 'Here's a simple way to eliminate afternoon fatigue forever'. For another good example of selling information, see the first sentence of this paragraph.

8. Get excited, *really* excited

Let's face it, information doesn't move people, emotions do. Make sure to punctuate your presentation with as much emotion as is possible and appropriate. Give yourself a pep talk before you go on. Tell yourself, 'I can't wait to get started. They're going to love me!' The more you stir the blood of the people you're addressing, the more they'll respond to you (although being powerful on the platform doesn't mean stomping around like a possessed Bolshevik). Look them in the eye, and don't hestitate to raise your voice — or even your fist — to make a point.

9. Talk simply, but talk fast

Make your sentences short and clear. Feel free to use jargon if you're talking to an audience that understands it ('speaking the language' of your audience increases rapport), but avoid it scrupulously if you think it has a chance of going over their heads. You'll lose them and possibly annoy them. If it's important to write simply in business (and it is), it's even more important to speak simply, because people can't go back and reread. They've got to understand it the first time.

Also, research shows that listeners have the ability to listen and comprehend two to three times as fast as most people speak. The result: listeners become understimulated, their minds wander, and they lose interest. Some tried-and-true ways of keeping an audience's interest include using visuals, moving around, and inviting audience participation. Another solution, somewhat less conventional, is to simply talk faster. Most people speak far more slowly than necessary, or desirable, before groups. One of our speakers just experienced a big upswing in her seminar evaluation ratings, and she attributes the improvement to talking faster. Talking in 'fast forward' without stumbling takes some practice, but if you can master it, you'll have a skill that could move you into the speakers' major leagues.

10. Use humour

Some people are dry, others silly, but we all have a humorous side that other people respond to. In presentations, lay it on. People love to laugh, and even more, they love to laugh in groups (that's why comedy films are so much funnier in a full theatre than they are when you play them on your video). Find out the kind of humour you can deliver best. If you can't tell a long joke, stick with one-liners (they don't require much timing and they're easy to remember). Or, best of all, just find the natural humour in what you're talking about. Don't make the mistake of thinking, 'This is too serious for humour'. Nothing is that serious. People laugh at funerals, world leaders tell jokes at summit meetings, trade union negotiators get slap-happy at the eleventh hour. Humour breaks the ice and cuts the tension.

11. Jump into the crowd

Don't hide behind a podium; it's a major psychological barrier between you and your audience. Have enough confidence in your talk to abandon your notes, at least for periods of time.

Then move around, point things out on your visuals, even walk
out into the crowd (one of the qualities that makes Bruce
Springsteen the performer's performer is that he leaps into the
crowd to sing and dance with his fans). Putting yourself out
there not only adds visual excitement, it shows you as relaxed
and in control.

12. Judge others

Critically assessing other speakers is probably your best way
to really appreciate what works and what doesn't in presentations. In Figure 17.1 we've reprinted a form, developed by one
of CareerTrack's trainers, J.J. Cochran, that will help you
organize your critiques of other presenters. The form identifies
the fifteen qualities that can make or break a presentation —
and a presenter. Use it the next time you go to see a public
speaker, sit through a sales presentation, or even watch a politi-
cian on television. It will put you in touch with the dos and
don'ts that will make you a better presenter.

THE TOTAL COMMUNICATION PACKAGE

APPEARANCE	1-------2-------3-------4-------5 ineffective, inappropriate	professional, powerful
CONFIDENCE	1-------2-------3-------4-------5 nervous, looks fearful	relaxed, has charisma
ENERGY	1-------2-------3-------4-------5 bored and boring	exuberant
VOICE MODULATION	1-------2-------3-------4-------5 monotone, little projection	varied rate, pitch, tone; easy to listen to
DICTION	1-------2-------3-------4-------5 choppy OR runs words together	polished
BODY MOVEMENT	1-------2-------3-------4-------5 stuck in one place OR pacing nervously	natural, comfortable, purposeful
GESTURES	1-------2-------3-------4-------5 rigid, none, confined OR too many	appropriate, natural, effective
FACIAL EXPRESSIONS	1-------2-------3-------4-------5 lifeless	vibrant, expressive, alive
EYE CONTACT	1-------2-------3-------4-------5 none, blank, avoids contact OR stares	looks at all parts of room, holds gaze without staring
ATTITUDE	1-------2-------3-------4-------5 apologetic OR talks down to others	equal with audience. positive
AUDIENCE PARTICIPATION	1-------2-------3-------4-------5 none OR inappropriate OR too much	effective, appropriate
HUMOUR	1-------2-------3-------4-------5 none OR ineffective OR inappropriate	effective, appropriate
EXPERTISE	1-------2-------3-------4-------5 doesn't know subject	in command of subject
CONTENT	1-------2-------3-------4-------5 disjointed, uninformed, outdated	easy to follow, stimulating
FINAL EFFECT	1-------2-------3-------4-------5 nothing new, unmotivating	educational, motivational

OTHER COMMENTS:

Figure 17.1   The total communication package

Overcome Conflict and Come Out Ahead

How to Turn Heat into Light

Blaming isn't changing.
— ROBERT M. BRAMSON

Conflict has got a bad reputation. All our lives we've heard messages such as 'don't fight', 'love one another', and 'be nice'. As a result we see conflict as a sign that somebody (usually the other side) is bad or wrong. Therefore, we try to avoid conflict, and sometimes simply pretend it doesn't exist. Ironically, this is precisely the attitude that creates more conflict.

While conflict can be painful, it is a natural, even healthy, part of life. That may be difficult to accept, but once you do, you are freed from having to blame a conflict on someone (whether yourself or others), which enables you to manage it more rationally — and productively.

Here's what we mean by overcoming conflict to come out ahead. First, minimize the amount of conflict in your life. Certain behaviours attract conflict like a magnet. When you identify and eliminate them, your life can become a lot easier.

Second, minimize the severity of your conflicts. Not every conflict needs to be escalated into World War III. Good conflict managers often find easy, painless resolutions to potentially explosive situations.

Third, win more. This requires a new definition of winning. Normally for there to be a winner there also has to be a loser; that's true in sports, politics, and war. But conflict management means finding a solution in which both sides can win. The downside is, you don't always get 100 per cent of what you want. Remember, however, that under the old 'win-lose' rules you often got 100 per cent of nothing.

The best reward for handling conflicts confidently is the way you feel about yourself. It seems that we have a choice in life: we can have conflicts either with other people or with ourselves. People who avoid external conflict by complying or pretending to be someone they're not usually end up raging with conflict inside. By bringing conflicts out in the open and overcoming them, we develop honest, forthright, and loving relationships with ourselves and others. We turn heat into light, and what could be better than that?

THE HOW-TO-DO-ITS

1. Choose time and place carefully

Never, ever initiate a conflict in a public setting or when uninvolved people are present. Also, be careful about confronting people after a hard day, before an event at which they have to be at their best (such as a presentation or performance review), when they are dealing with a mistake or loss, or when they're working under a deadline. Sensitivity to the other person's circumstances is important in any one-to-one communication, but in a conflict it is critical.

2. Change behaviours, not people

There are two directions in which you can go when facing a conflict: firstly, you can fix the problem; or secondly, you can fix the blame. The first is by far the more productive. If you make it your goal in a conflict to convince the other person that he or she is wrong or bad, you will almost certainly fail. How much better it is simply to change that person's negative behaviour. Sometimes this may even require applying pressure, as in the following example.

A couple of years ago, when Warner Books purchased the rights to our first book, *Real World 101*, Warner's art director, Charles, designed a cover which we didn't feel was appropriate. It was cartoonish and misrepresented the book, and we were convinced it would kill sales. So Jeff called Charles to persuade him to change it. When Jeff had finished explaining his point of view, Charles *hung up on him.* (That's really not so surprising; when it comes to the issue of marketing, most publishers hold a thinly veiled contempt for authors.)

It was obvious Jeff wasn't going to get anywhere with Charles, so he decided to go over Charles's head. Jeff spent the rest of the day at his trusty word processor, drafting what turned out to be a three-page, single-spaced letter, detailing the reasons why the cover should be changed. Copies of the letter went out to our editor; the president of Warner Books; and the art director, Charles. Jeff didn't mention the phone call — there was no point in making Charles even more defensive than he already was.

Jeff sent the letters in three separate overnight express packages so he'd know exactly when they arrived — and the recipients would know he knew. He also made it clear to each that copies had been sent to the others, so the matter would be dealt with quickly.

It worked. About two hours after his letters had been delivered, Jeff's secretary announced that Warner's art director was on the phone. Answering Jeff said, 'Hi, Charles', in his most unassuming voice. Charles said, 'Jeff, you write a great letter. You'll have your new cover in two weeks'. He also mumbled some explanation that seemed vaguely to blame the editor for the earlier cover. Jeff saw through this flimsy excuse but didn't argue. He simply said, 'Thanks, Charles, I really appreciate your co-operation'.

The point is, don't quit; and if you really care a lot, don't take no for an answer until you've exhausted every avenue. And above all, don't spend your time making someone 'wrong' when all you really want is to change his or her behaviour.

Here's another example: If you have a typist who consistently misspells words, you may be tempted to point out that 'good typists would never make these mistakes', a claim that would certainly be 'right'. Two more productive resolutions, however, would be, firstly, to buy your typist a speller's dictionary or, better yet, buy a typewriter or word processor that identifies misspelled words. The key is to keep your eye on the solution, not on the problem.

3. Agree on something

Restating your agreement on basic goals makes it easier to discuss your disagreements on how to achieve them. It reminds both sides that the relationship is solid (which instantly

minimizes insecurity and defensiveness) and sets the stage for
co-operation and problem-solving — you're on the same side
instead of being adversaries. A couple of ways to state your
agreement on basic goals are: 'I'm bringing this up because
I believe in you and want you to succeed here', and 'It seems
we agree that we need to get this project done by the end of
the month'.

4. Use 'I–language'

'I–language' means stating your case in terms of your own feelings. For instance, instead of telling someone, 'You broke our
agreement', you would say, 'I'm not happy with the way things
are going with our agreement'. Notice how the first comment
('you-language') naturally leads to defensiveness — it is, after
all, an attack. The second statement may not be welcomed by
the other person, but it is far more likely to be accepted. Make
I–language your approach even on minor issues. For instance,
say, 'I didn't understand what you said', instead of 'You didn't
explain that clearly'. By forcing you to keep your argument
to the facts and preventing personal attacks, I–language serves
you on all three conflict-management fronts: it reduces the
number of conflicts, minimizes their severity, and leads more
easily to winning solutions.

5. Figure out where you went wrong . . .

. . . or how you may have contributed to the conflict, and admit
it. Difficult as this is, owning up to your mistakes is one of
the most important aspects of conflict management. Did your
rushed directions contribute to your secretary's mishandling
of an issue? If so, admit it early on and you'll free the other
person to admit his or her part in the problem. When appropriate
(and that's probably more often than you think), there's no better
way to start a confrontation than to say, 'I know I'm partly
responsible for this situation.'

6. Criticize with precision

A lot of conflict is the result of sloppy and vague criticism.
Say you tell one of your employees, 'You're unprofessional'.
Unless that person knows what you mean by unprofessional,
there's not much he or she can do about it — except feel bad,

resentful, unmotivated, spiteful . . . do you get the picture? How much better it is to point out specifically: 'Punctuality is important to me and you were twenty minutes late this morning and ten minutes late for this appointment'. Conversely, when someone gives you vague criticism, ask that it be clarified: 'What am I doing that makes you think I'm unprofessional? I'd like to change it.' Think about this the next time you tell someone (or someone tells you), 'You have a bad attitude', 'Your performance isn't up to par', or any one of the many vague criticisms that we hear every day.

7. When someone attacks . . . agree

On occasion you may find yourself dealing with someone whose goal is to hurt you or to embarrass you in public. Trying to find a 'win-win' solution will not work, because his or her goal is to make you lose. In a case like this, some creative side-stepping may be in order. For example, if someone says, 'Your tie clashes with your suit', your response might be 'You're right, my tie *does* clash with my suit'. By refusing to acknowledge the sniper's implicit attack — 'You don't know how to dress, you're unprofessional, you don't belong here, etc.' — you have deflected it. In fact your implied message is 'So what?' — a retort your attacker will rarely counter.

Another way to handle the person who insults you in public is simply to look him or her in the eye for a second or so . . . then move on. Your implied message in this case is 'I heard what you said, and I'm not going to deal with it'. Not dealing with it is a right you can exercise most effectively to leave the insult in the sniper's lap, where it belongs. Be careful that you don't come across as pretending you didn't hear the insult. That's power*less* behaviour. Make sure the eye contact is strong and confident before you move on.

8. Bow out for a while

Giving yourself time is a good rule of thumb in all conflicts, but it's particularly important in high-emotion situations. Time allows the emotions to cool, which enables both sides to move more easily from the blame phase to the solution stage. Imagine that you have discovered, to your outrage, that an associate has overstepped his or her bounds and caused a big problem for you. Instead of confronting your associate immediately, force yourself to wait a few hours or even a day. This doesn't mean you shouldn't have a strong confrontation, just that you'll be more effective once the first rush of anger has subsided.

9. Have *more* conflicts

Many people, believing that conflict is a sign of a major break-down in a relationship, strive to have conflict-free relationships. To do that they avoid, or swallow, the inevitable problems that do arise between people. As a result resentment builds, either slowly undermining the positive aspects of the relationship or instantly causing an explosion. How much better it is to bring up problems and annoyances — even minor ones — as they happen. Some people may find this behaviour odd at first, but they will come to appreciate the result: a relationship where honesty prevails and neither side keeps an 'account' against the other.

10. Find the third option

The minute emotions flare, the natural inclination is for both sides to lock into their positions automatically. The goodwill is gone, and the goal is no longer to resolve the conflict; it is *to win*. This is a critical juncture, and how you handle it determines whether you will be a winner or a loser at managing conflict. The challenge is to break out of the 'win-lose' bind.

Two married friends of ours tell of the evening when it was the husband's turn to cook. He didn't feel like it, so he suggested that they go out to dinner. His wife was tired and she refused. Just as each was getting into how selfish and insensitive the other was, their four-year-old daughter suggested having a pizza delivered. End of argument. Creative solutions are often embarrassingly easy to find. Just be open to them.

11. Agree on the future

Just as it is helpful to keep your conflict focused on the specifics of the problem, it pays to keep the solution focused on the specific *action* that will be taken. Say, for instance, your boss confronts you on exceeding your budget on a project. Instead of saying something like, 'I'll be more careful next time', you might suggest that you present weekly budget updates on your next project. By agreeing to this specific course of action (instead of just stating your good intentions), you demonstrate your commitment to solving the problem and dramatically decrease the chances of its happening again.

12. Work it out on paper

A tool that integrates many of the principles we've just presented is reproduced in Figure 18.1. It's a simple conflict worksheet that we use in some of our seminars. The beauty of the system, as with all good systems, is its simplicity. If you invest the two minutes it takes to complete this form, you are far more likely to get positive results in your next conflict. The letters below correspond to the letters on the form:

A. *Describe the results of the other person's negative behaviour.* Either describe your feelings ('I get angry') or the bottom-line effect in terms of time, money, morale, etc. ('It causes us all to miss our deadlines').

B. *Describe the other person's negative behaviour.* Remember to focus on the behaviour, not the person ('When you miss your deadlines' or 'When you raise your voice', not 'When you act like an idiot'). Remember to be specific and non-judgemental.

C. *Make a request.* Identify the preferred behaviour and ask the person to use it ('Would you please be more realistic about your deadlines').

D. *Describe the positive effect of co-operating.* This is the benefit to the person if he or she changes the negative behaviour ('I'm sure we could work together much better').

E. *Describe the negative effect of not co-operating* (optional). ('I'm going to have to give you a written warning next time you're late'.) Be specific about the follow-through, then do it. As the song says, don't make promises you can't keep.

Photocopy this form and keep it handy.

CONFLICT WORKSHEET

A. I (or it) _____

_____

B. When you _____

_____

C. Would you please _____

_____

D. If you do _____

_____

E. If you don't _____

Optional, use only if positive effect has failed.

_____

Figure 18.1   Conflict worksheet

Negotiate Better Deals

Everything Is Negotiable

You've got to give a little ... take a little.
— BILLY HILL, 'THE GLORY OF LOVE'

Nobody accepts a bad deal. Or do they? Sometimes a good deal turns out to be a bad one, such as when people discover they paid too much. Then they're out to even the score, whether that means backing out or honouring an agreement with the least possible commitment.

This illustrates the major problem — and opportunity — of negotiating. For a deal to be good, it must benefit both sides; that way both sides are invested in making it work. Yet nobody wants to pay a penny more than he or she has to, and rightly so.

It's a tightrope to walk. Here are two keys to balancing these conflicting goals. The first is collaboration, which means making more pie so both sides can have a bigger piece. Collaboration is negotiation at its most sophisticated — and best. Here's an example: you're negotiating to buy a house, but you and the seller are $5000 apart. If you don't get stuck on the price argument, you may find that the seller is willing to leave the furniture for $5000. You would have had to spend twice that to furnish the house, and the buyer was moving overseas and couldn't use the furniture anyway. You're both big winners. Collaboration is why most good negotiators like to deal with other good negotiators — they're more open to creative, pie-enlarging solutions.

The second key is compromise. This isn't nearly as desirable as collaboration, but it can get you an acceptable-to-good deal when you can't find any creative solutions, or you're dealing with someone who is unwilling to participate in trying to find them. Compromise means trading concessions: the seller wants $1000, you want to pay $800, you compromise at $900. True, both sides end up with less than they wanted, but remember, 90 per cent of something is better than 100 per cent of nothing. To compromise effectively, you must really examine your position to separate the 'must haves' from the 'would like to haves'. Are your non-negotiables reasonable, or emotional and ego-driven? How about theirs? Don't give away the ship, just the parts you don't need to keep afloat. Expect no more from them.

Keep these two points, collaboration and compromise, in mind, along with the following twelve how-to-do-its, and you'll make better deals more consistently.

THE HOW-TO-DO-ITS

1. Know what you want

Don't underestimate the power of being committed to what you want. Identify your goal *specifically*, with numbers and dates, if appropriate. Remember, many people undermine their power by going into a negotiation wanting 'the best deal' or 'as much as I can get'. Such vague goals are powerless because the minute the negotiation takes an unexpected tack, you have no anchor. With clear objectives, you will add to your confidence by knowing that you deserve what you want, and by visualizing having successfully negotiated it.

When Jimmy negotiated the lease on our current office space, he knew that there was a surplus of empty offices and that a 'good deal' could be had. In better times office space was selling at $12 per square foot, but $10, or less, leases had become available. Based on the depressed commercial real-estate market and some quick research, Jimmy decided that $9 was the most we needed to pay.

After finding the perfect building (with an asking price of $11.50), Jimmy made an offer of $9 per square foot. The owners snickered and countered with $10. Jimmy resubmitted his original $9 offer... and the owners countered at $9.50. Jimmy again resubmitted his original $9 offer. Realizing Jimmy was unyielding and perfectly willing to look elsewhere, the owners finally accepted at $9 and a deal was struck.

The lesson: the more clearly you have defined your position and the more strongly you have committed yourself to it, the more likely you are to get what you want.

2. Identify the person who can say yes

Virtually anyone in an organization can say no to deals. In fact, many people will negotiate with you even though they know they are not empowered to say yes. Why? To perpetuate an illusion (to you and, strangely enough, to themselves) of having power. Moreover, by saying no they ensure that 'the way it's always been done' will continue to be the way it is done. Their 'no' decisions make people's lives easier — after all, saying yes means somebody's got to do something.

The point is, your chances for successfully negotiating a deal dramatically increase if you can present your offer to a decision-maker who can say, 'Yes, we'll do it'. One reason is that a high-ranking decision-maker must justify the time he or she spends negotiating. Investing hours, days, or weeks at the bargaining table only to come away empty handed is perceived as a waste of expensive executive time.

So how do you determine if the person you're dealing with can make an agreement? Simple — just ask: 'Do you have the authority to make this agreement?' Few people will respond with an out-and-out lie. Most will answer, 'Well, of course, I have to get my boss's approval' or some committee's approval, etc. Now you have important information: you're not dealing with the person in power. In this case ask if it's OK to send the 'higher power' photocopies of proposals, memos, etc. See if you can get an appointment with him, her, or them. Do whatever you can to get information on your proposed deal into their hands and in front of their eyes. At least make sure you arm your contact with all the features and benefits necessary for him or her to sell upper management on the merits of your deal.

3. Extend yourself first

When CareerTrack was approached to produce the one-day, public-seminar version of an all-time best-selling management book, *The One Minute Manager*, co-author Ken Blanchard invited Jimmy to fly out to his corporate headquarters to 'talk'. Expecting a typical business meeting/negotiation, Jimmy was surprised when he was asked to stay at Ken's home instead of a hotel. Thinking this was unusual, he was slightly suspicious. Ken did a few other unexpected things — he personally met

Jimmy at the airport, stayed up late talking about the thesis of his next book, and the next evening drove Jimmy an hour out of his way to meet a friend.

But that's not what most impressed Jimmy. Rather, it was Ken's reaction to a stranded motorist they encountered shortly after leaving the airport. Ninety-nine per cent of all people drive past unfortunate motorists in such predicaments. Not Ken. Upon spotting a woman in a broken-down car in the middle of an intersection, Ken immediately pulled over his Mercedes, gave the let's-give-her-a-hand signal to Jimmy, and the two of them pushed the woman's car into a vacant parking lot. Then Ken offered to let her call for help from his car phone, saving her from having to search for a pay phone in the dark. But that wasn't all. Not wanting to leave the woman alone in a remote part of town, waiting for her friend, Ken suggested that she come along with them to a restaurant and wait there. 'It would be safer,' he said.

Ken wasn't through yet. When they arrived, he asked the woman to join them for a cocktail until her friend arrived, and then offered to send her an autographed copy of his book. Jimmy couldn't believe his eyes or ears — was this guy for real? Before he had known Ken for an hour or negotiated one item on his agenda, Jimmy knew he was about to do business with an unusually generous and kind man. Having seen Ken extend himself to a businessman he had never met, and then to a total stranger in need, Jimmy found himself trusting and liking the author from the start. And he was motivated to arrange what was a complex deal in a relatively short period of time.

Most people *do* appreciate the value of a co-operative, trusting relationship. But, often, even people who appreciate the value of these relationships don't know quite how to go about negotiating one. It's human nature to approach another person with suspicion. Anyone who has lived in the real world any length of time knows firsthand that people can be very dangerous. So when you're trying to negotiate a co-operative relationship with someone, don't be surprised if you run into initial hesitation. The implicit demand is: 'You first. You extend yourself to me and I'll extend myself to you.'

When you run into this attitude — and you will, a lot —

our advice is to take the person up on it! Go ahead and be the first to extend yourself. The worst that could happen is that they will take advantage of you. Or you may find that they are not sufficiently experienced to handle a co-operative relationship. Either way it's probably not the end of the world; many relationships that start out badly turn into productive, creative, enjoyable, and lasting partnerships. Provided you're not risking too much initially, it's worth the risk. In fact, it's the only way to go. Once personal bonds begin to form, both sides naturally take an interest in the other's well-being, and they will do business happily ever after (at least most of the time).

4. Play fair

As they say in the stock market, you can be a bear or a bull, but not a pig. Getting a good deal does not mean defeating the other side. The quickest way to sabotage a negotiation — and with it a relationship — is to push too hard to try to get something for nothing. Get rid of the notion that in order to succeed in a negotiation you have to gain the better deal. You may have scored by taking advantage of another person, but you have also created a person who is intent on evening the score. That means you'll have to bear the long-term burden of keeping up your guard — and ultimately you will have paid very dearly for your 'advantage'.

Uncooperative relationships can endure, but they never work very well. They are too riddled with rules, suspicion, selfishness, and inflexibility to be productive. Surprisingly, though, many people feel that this is the way business ought to be done. They feel if a person they are dealing with isn't at least slightly resentful of them, then they must not be getting the best deal.

5. Solve the other side's problems first

Unfortunately, most people begin by laying out *their* problems, demands, non-negotiables, and 'take it or leave its'. How much better it is to demonstrate your commitment to solving your opponents' problems. When you do this you can sit back and watch them solve yours — because they want to ensure that you'll follow through on your end of the bargain. You'll also earn a reputation for being fair and pleasant to deal with. And, in the long run, that will bring you even better deals.

A purchasing agent we know once negotiated an incredible deal on several thousand cardboard boxes after hearing that a particular supplier had just bought a new fabrication machine and was experiencing a tight cash flow. Recognizing the supplier's predicament, she offered to prepay the entire job in exchange for a faster turnaround time and a substantial price reduction. The manufacturers obviously saw this as a solution to their problem, because they quickly accepted the offer. When you look at every deal from the perspective of what problems the other side might be facing — and how you can solve them — you'll make more lucrative deals.

6. Sell the future

Most deals are part of a long string of deals. Make sure your negotiating opponent sees the long-term benefits of striking a deal *this* time. Otherwise people see each negotiation as a 'must-win' situation and get stingy with concessions. A proven way to move the other side is to talk about the potential (or lack thereof) for future deals.

Our data-processing director, Jim, uses this strategy when negotiating with sellers of computer hardware. Whenever he reaches a stalemate on price, Jim reminds the salesperson of our company's projected growth and likely need for more equipment in the future. This implied promise cajoles salespeople into giving us a good deal now in exchange for the possibility of more sales later on. It allows them to justify giving in on the price without looking like pushovers.

Another proven method of selling the future is to use 'policy'. Once our company establishes a standard price on frequently ordered supplies and services, we inform suppliers that it's our policy to continue buying from them unless one of three things happens: 1   their service slips; 2   their quality deteriorates; or 3   they raise the price. In fact, we tell them in advance that any price increase will trigger us to solicit bids from other suppliers. This 'policy' deters suppliers from arbitrarily charging us with price increases, and it keeps them on their toes with regard to quality and service. It's amazing how well this 'policy' sticks in our suppliers' minds.

7. Stick to the issues

Occasionally you will run into an opponent who uses threats, bullying tactics, and deception. He or she could be: 1 Deliberately trying to rattle you. *Response:* Smile knowingly; it's only a game. 2 Temporarily out of control emotionally. *Response:* Keep dragging the conversation back to specific issues. 3 Basically mean-spirited. *Response:* Run the other way as fast as you can; you don't need a deal that badly. In any case, resist an impulse to return the same treatment. Emotional outbursts will only divide you and prolong the process. Besides, it's considered to be bad business practice.

The tough part is dragging the discussion back to the issues. When somebody gets personal it's very difficult not to become defensive or, worse, bite the bait and start returning insults. Our attorney, Bob Purcell, taught us how to avoid this trap. A few years ago we were involved in a lawsuit settlement. During the negotiation, the opposing lawyer began ranting and raving, attempting to intimidate Bob into accepting a lesser deal. This person was downright nasty, raising all kinds of superfluous issues and insulting Bob's competence. We sat there incensed (we weren't allowed to say a word), and it was all we could do not to stand up and shout, 'To hell with you, we'll see you in court!'

Bob's response? He ignored the other side's offensive behaviour and kept restating our bottom-line settlement offer. After a few rounds it became obvious that we weren't going to budge, emotionally or substantively. Our opponent instructed his attorney to accept our offer.

Afterwards we asked Bob how he had managed to keep cool. He gave us the long-suffering look one gives young innocents like we were, and said simply, 'Oh, it's all part of the game'. On the way out of the courthouse we passed the opposing attorney in the hall. The two of us wanted to run up to him and jeer, but Bob beat us to it. He said, 'See you around, Mike'. The other attorney smiled and said, 'OK, Bob, have a good weekend'.

What a game!

8. Don't avoid emotional appeals

Some people operate under the delusion that business is

'businesslike' and all business deals should be limited to numbers, dates, and bottom lines. Nonsense! Business involves people, and people are motivated by emotions. For example, look at the breakthrough moment in the Camp David peace accords. After days of refereeing fruitless negotiations between Begin and Sadat, President Carter visited Begin privately and offered to autograph his photo for Begin's grandchildren. Begin began to cry as he thought about the future world in which his grandchildren would live. The next day he conceded on some key issues, prompting Sadat to do the same. The result: peace between two nations. The moral: When you hit a brick wall, consider climbing over it or digging a tunnel beneath.

9. Don't accept too quickly

Ever made an offer on a used car and had the seller say yes immediately? Then you know the feeling of 'I paid too much'. People need to be assured that a deal was fought for and won, because any negotiation that happens too fast leaves one side feeling unsatisfied. When selling, always make a counteroffer (no matter how sweet the initial offer), just to make the buyer confident he or she got your best price. When buying, always offer less than you'd be willing to pay, just so the seller can think he or she got the best deal.

Here's an example of a deal that was made too quickly. One Sunday morning, not long after we had started Career-Track, Jeff encountered a crisis. A trainer who was scheduled to present a seminar the next day called from the hospital to say she was too sick to give the programme. Since it was Sunday and we didn't have our customers' home phone numbers, there was no way we could cancel the seminar. Then Jeff remembered that we had another trainer who gave the exact programme in another region of the country.

He called her immediately and asked, 'Jane, can you be on a plane to Pittsburgh, Pennsylvania at three o'clock this afternoon?'

She thought for a minute and came back with a firm, 'Maybe'.

Jeff got the picture. He said, 'Okay Jane, *what would it take* for you to be on a plane to Pittsburgh at three o'clock this afternoon?'

She said, 'An extra $200.'

Jeff was thrilled. Another crisis averted! He was so happy he said, 'I'll give you $300'.

Jeff expected her to shriek with joy. But she didn't. Instead she said, 'Well, it is awfully short notice'.

She wasn't happy. In fact, she was kicking herself for not having asked for $400 or $500. She was wondering, 'Just how desperate is he?'

Jeff realizes now how much better it would have turned out if he had balked at her first $200 request, and perhaps negotiated her down, or at least fought for a while before accepting it. Then after she had given the programme he could have sent her $300 with a note saying, 'Here's a little bonus for helping us out in a pinch.'

Notice that either way the cost would have been $300, but the second option would have strengthened the relationship. People need to feel that they *earned* what they won in a negotiation. Don't deprive them of that feeling by accepting too quickly.

10. Make sure your opponent has competition

When you let the person with whom you are negotiating know someone else is after your business, he or she is far more motivated to give you the best possible deal.

When we purchased a quarter-of-a-million dollar phone system, we unknowingly used this strategy to obtain a $20 000 price concession. Our telecommunications manager, Jeanne, had spent months researching the leading phone systems and recommended the AT&T System 75. Because our company had previously purchased three AT&T systems, AT&T was undoubtedly feeling that it had our account tied up and could stand firm on its quoted price. And given that we (the decision task force) had all shown our enthusiasm over the System 75, our bargaining position wasn't exactly what you'd call strong. But then something unusual happened.

The day before the purchase order was to be signed, a competitive phone company representative called Jimmy at home to make a last-ditch effort to steal the sale from AT&T. He pointed out that his system cost $100 000 less and would perform more functions than the AT&T system, so naturally Jimmy's curiosity was aroused. Jimmy subsequently called Jeanne, told her to put a hold on the AT&T system, and asked her to review the competitor's written proposal. Having spent considerable time and effort researching the best phone system, Jeanne feared her recommendation was about to be ignored. And, to make matters worse, she was the one who would have to work with the alternative system, which she deemed inferior.

Sensing she needed to do something dramatic to save the AT&T deal, Jeanne called her AT&T salesperson and told him that a competitor had called her boss at home and captured his attention, and that Jimmy was now leaning towards the competitor's system. AT&T was alarmed (newly denationalized, it wasn't accustomed to competition), and asked what it would take to clinch the deal immediately. Jeanne suggested a substantial price discount to 'recapture Jimmy's attention'. AT&T quickly agreed to knock off $20 000 by offering free add-ons, service, and installation. The power of competition!

11. Swim in small ponds

Want a better deal? Then deal with the people who will most value your patronage. Smaller, growing companies will often make you a better deal because they are hungrier, have lower overheads, and maybe even need your account just to survive.

This tip is particularly useful for small- and medium-sized businesses which are supplier-driven, that is, whose success hinges on timely delivery of consistently high-quality goods and services. If you fit into this category (most companies do), then we suggest that you generally avoid working with 'giant' suppliers. It's not that smaller suppliers will say 'how high' when you say 'jump', but your account will probably get more attention, simply because they have fewer customers.

At CareerTrack we print and mail over 40 million brochures and catalogues each year to advertise our training programmes. Although this volume qualifies us as a 'major client' even by a large printer's standards, we have always preferred to work with mid-size printers. We enjoy the special treatment that comes with being one of their most important and valued clients.

12. Never buy when you must

It's your worst possible time, because a pressing need always clouds your objectivity. Ever shopped for a car months before you were ready to buy one and turned down the salesperson's 'best' offer, only to have him or her call you the next day with a much better one? When you're clearly in need, a salesperson is not motivated to reach his or her bottom-line price. If you don't have the luxury of shopping well in advance, then at least feign a lack of urgency.

And don't forget to honour the Five Per Cent Rule. An old salesperson's trick is to say, 'Better buy now; it may be gone tomorrow'. If you really want an item, the thought of losing it can be intimidating. But remember, there's only a 5 per cent likelihood it will sell before you're back (seldom is there a second buyer ready to lay his or her money down). In almost all cases, you can walk away and buy later — and often get a better deal.

In summary, here are seven dos and don'ts to ensure that you negotiate better deals: 1   *Do* your homework and get all the facts before you sit down — knowledge is power. 2   *Do* put everything in writing — poor memories have ruined many otherwise good deals. 3   *Do* be willing to walk away — and make sure the other side knows it. 4   *Do* follow through — remember, implementing an agreement is just as important as negotiating it. 5   *Don't* rush a deal — the longer the negotiation, the more invested your opponent will be in coming to agreement. 6   *Don't* take a bad deal — you'll regret it. 7   *Don't* force a bad deal — it will come back to haunt you.

Move from Management to Leadership

Take Charge

*The elusive half-step between middle management
and true leadership is grace under pressure.*
— JOHN F. KENNEDY

Some benefits of leadership are obvious. If you're an effective leader, then you have more people and power behind you to make things happen.

But you can get what you want, at least to a degree, simply through good management. Leadership is something more. It's a calling, and most satisfying on a non-material level. In fact, leadership is best appreciated, not as a means of gaining something, but as a means of contributing something. Therefore, leadership is not so much a matter of what you do. What you do is management. Leadership is more abstract, more a matter of how you think. If you think the right way, you'll do the right things automatically.

As a leader you have a very special relationship with your staff. You're in charge of giving them direction, helping them find out who they are, and supporting them to perform at levels they didn't know they could reach. For this reason, leadership is not a responsibility to be taken lightly. You must remember that your staff are not your servants, they're not your toys, they're not machines. They're human beings who, consciously or not, have entrusted a significant part of their lives to you.

We see great leaders in all areas of life. Some are at the helms of large corporations, some are supervisors of small departments within large corporations, some are in charge of Scout troops. Some are charismatic and larger than life, and others are quietly effective.

The variety of leaders is good news, because it shows leadership can be exercised by virtually anyone who 'has the calling' and takes the time to learn and practise it. If you develop the qualities identified in this chapter, you will be well on your way to becoming a great leader.

THE HOW-TO-DO-ITS

1. Have a vision

It must be a clear vision of what the organization and the individuals in it will be like in the future. The key is that it be simple, appealing, and memorable. In many cases your staff won't have a clear vision of their own lives. A lot of managers write these people off. A good leader, however, makes it his or her job to help them find their goals and become committed to them. It's wonderful to turn people on in this way, and it's something for which they are eternally grateful.

2. Let people see how they contribute to the vision

Every step of the way. Nobody gets fired up to work on an assembly line. That's because they are isolated from the finished product and, therefore, deprived of taking pride in it. There are three ways to minimize the 'assembly-line' characteristics of the jobs your staff perform: 1 broaden the job so they can handle one task from beginning to end; 2 vary the part they play in completing the task, so they can have a working understanding of the whole; and 3 show them constantly how their jobs, and your department, are contributing to the company's overall goals.

Well, you may say, it's easy to create a vision if you run a computer firm — you're freeing people from drudgery. But how do you create a vision for people who are serving hamburgers, for instance?

Jeff has a friend in Florida who owns a couple of Burger King franchises. He has a vision for his restaurants, which he constantly reiterates to every employee and which is reflected in every employee and which is reflected in every decision he makes. He says to his staff, 'Life is tough. It's hot out there; people are sitting in traffic jams, breathing fumes and sweating. Their budgets are strained, their marriages are rotten, and their kids are rebelling. It's a world of trouble out there, and I want this Burger King to be a respite from the storm, an oasis for the tired traveller. I want the food hot, the air cool, the corners clean, and the people friendly here, so for half an hour customers can come in and have a nice experience.'

That's that. His employees are motivated by that message. That's *vision*.

3. Exude energy
It's magnetic. High energy is a well-known characteristic of super-achievers in all fields. Strong leaders always project optimism and confidence. While they are skilled at creating various moods in the organization, they are not themselves moody. Their 'can-do' demeanour energizes others to stretch themselves, to tackle the toughest jobs, to beat the odds, and to win.

4. Help your staff reach *their* goals
Not just *your* goals. The trick is to find where your staff's goals and your goals overlap, and concentrate there. Occasionally it means supporting them in something you don't agree with. If they're very enthusiastic, you've got to let them try it and find out for themselves. It may turn out that *you* were wrong. If that happens, great. You can freely admit it, admire them for persisting, and get behind the idea with all your might. Now that's good leadership. (Good leaders aren't always right, but they're always open to being convinced.)

5. Promote your staff
A key part of your job as a leader is supporting your staff's rise to the top. You must consistently promote your staff within your organization, industry, and community. Photocopy positive reviews and written acknowledgements and send them to upper management. Talk to your staff formally in company news-letters, and informally among your fellow leaders. For pro-motions and significant accomplishments, send a short press release to your community newspaper. Few things better build commitment in your staff than knowing that you are actively supporting their success.

6. Give yourself permission to lead
A significant barrier new leaders often have to overcome is

the discomfort of having control over another person's life. It *can* be unsettling at first, but it *is* necessary.

Jeff is reminded of a poster he saw by an ageing hippie secretary's desk; it said, 'You do your thing and I'll do my thing, and if somehow we should come together, that's beautiful'. It's a lovely thought; unfortunately, it doesn't work in business. As a leader you may have to say no to your secretary's request for a well-deserved afternoon off, because there's one more task that must be done that day. You may even determine how much money another person earns — how could you insert yourself into their lives more than that? You must become comfortable with doing just that. As long as leadership power is exercised fairly, people will accept it.

7. Give yourself time to lead

One problem aspiring leaders face is that they don't allow themselves time to lead. Most people got promoted to a leadership position because they were good workers. To them the 'soft' functions of a leader — creating vision, praising, coaching — don't feel like work. But they are essential to leadership success. So make sure you set aside a portion of your day for nothing more than being with your staff, hearing their problems, reinforcing the 'vision', and letting them know you care.

It may help to formalize the process so that you are certain to implement it. That's worked well for the two of us. A couple of years ago, when our company began its major growth spurt, we became concerned that, as founders and leaders of the company, we were falling out of touch with the new people who were being employed. When the company was smaller, it was easy and natural for us to have flesh-and-blood contact with every new employee — truth be told, we generally employed and worked with them personally.

We came up with two solutions. First we implemented a 'new employee luncheon', where newly-employed people could sit down with us and talk informally. The luncheons are small: eight new employees and the two of us. We hold a luncheon every time we've eight new staff; sometime it's once a month, sometimes it's once a quarter. True, the luncheons were designed to show new CareerTrackers how we think and what our plans for the company are, but it's turned out to be just as valuable for the insight it gives us into the views of a new person just entering our company. In fact, we now have a system: we go around the table, asking each person to give his or her first impressions of CareerTrack, contrast it with other places they've worked, and suggest ways for us to help new employees acclimatize We generally have to push to get them to say anything other than an eager-to-please 'CareerTrack is great!' but eventually they open up. As a result we never leave a luncheon without gaining insights and ideas that we can use to help future new employees settle in even quicker.

The second solution we came up with for keeping in touch with recently employed people is the 'new employee orientation'. We hold an orientation every three months, for as many new people as joined in that period. In the orientation we give the history of the company (we use a funny slide show to set an upbeat tone for the meeting), an explanation of how it operates, an overview of our industry, and our vision for the company. That's a lot to cover, and it can take up to three hours. But we feel it's one of the best possible uses of our time. Leaders must have contact with their staff, they must take the time to share their vision, and they must let their people know they care enough to take the time. And, needless to say, that applies to everyone, no matter how long they've been with the company.

8. Become a communicator

As you well know, it's not always what you say that counts — it's how you say it. This is particularly true of leaders. A good leader is always a good communicator, one-to-one and with groups. Make it a point to develop the skills of writing, speaking, reading, and especially listening. As you'll remember from Success Shortcut 11, powerful listening means not only being open to bad news, but sometimes soliciting it. At CareerTrack we have systematized the process with the form shown in Figure 20.1. We give this form to our staff every now and then, whenever we want a morale check.

9. Be decisive . . .

As we noted in Success Shortcut 10, one of the paradoxes of success is that it is often more important to be decisive than right. Being decisive gives you leadership power in two ways.

CONFIDENTIAL FEEDBACK FORM

Date: _____

Name (optional): _____

You know better than we do how you can be happier, less hassled, and more productive. Now you can tell us, and remain anonymous if you'd like. Please take the time to fill this out and return it to us by (date). Hold nothing back: This is your golden opportunity to make (company or department) a better place to work.

The tasks I perform that seem to have little value:

Where I see duplication of effort:

The annoying or demeaning rules/forms/procedures I would eliminate:

If I were in charge of my department, I would change:

If I were managing director of my organization, I would change:

The best thing about working here is:

Figure 20.1   Confidential feedback form

First, it always makes you a more formidable foe. Second, it engenders support. Most people are dying to make a commitment to their work. They are more than willing to follow someone who has a clear, decisive direction.

. . . yet flexible

The strength of decisiveness must be tempered by flexibility. The idea of being strong yet flexible is often confusing to leaders. Yet it's really quite simple. Where a leader must be unbending is in the overall values and goals of the organization. Where he or she must be flexible is in the tactics for achieving them. As Thomas Jefferson said, 'In matters of style, swim with the current; in matters of principle, stand like a rock.'

10. Be the eye of the hurricane

When things go wrong, you have two possible responses: first, you can turn your attention to assigning the blame, or second, turn your attention to solving the problem. It's been shown that good leaders choose the second, and they do it calmly and deliberately. In times of crisis people need a solid, confident presence to lean on. We know this advice is easier to read than to act upon. However, a good rule of thumb is to wait twenty-four hours (or at least one hour, if you're coming unstuck) before you approach anyone about the crisis at hand.

11. Get in up to your elbows

A leader cannot lead from above the battlefield. Your staff need to see you working as hard as they are. The way to demonstrate that details are important, for instance, is by paying attention to details yourself. Also, your staff must be able to approach you as a person. Relax with them, laugh with them, *be* with them. In the big picture, all people are equal. If you demonstrate through your behaviour that you are somehow above certain things, you will risk undermining your people's commitment to you.

12. Demand excellence

The danger in emphasizing positive reinforcement in management is that it downplays the power of toughness and discipline.

To see someone doing something wrong and not correct the mistake is just another way of showing you don't care. More people are inspired by knowing that their leader believes in their excellence and won't accept anything less from them. The key as a leader is to demand excellence for *their* sake, not just yours or the organization's. Keep the spotlight turned on one area for improvement at a time. Make your feedback immediate; people need to know how they're doing *now*.

And don't act like royalty (it's tempting when you're in the power position). Admit your own weaknesses, and show how you're demanding excellence from yourself as well. One way to dramatize this is to conduct a reverse performance evaluation. Asking your people how you are doing will reinforce their perception of you as a leader open to criticism and improvement.

The best way we've found for measuring and improving your leadership abilities is the reverse performance appraisal we have created at CareerTrack (see Figure 20.2). At CareerTrack, each level of management distributes this simple form every six months to the people they supervise. The one rule we insist on is that no manager can show his or her appraisals to anyone higher in the organization without the permission of the employee who filled it out. This helps ensure that employees feel free to be honest in their evaluations without feeling like tell-tales, and managers are more open to the criticism because they don't have to defend their 'report cards' to those higher up.

When you hand out the forms, be sure to ask for specific examples in the 'Comments' section next to the performance factors. Then, when you're reading through your appraisals, we suggest making comments on top of your employees' comments, such as 'How can I improve?' 'Why do I deserve this grade?' or 'Give me an example'. Don't settle for vague praise or harsh criticism without actual instances to justify them. Keep the form going back and forth until you have a thorough understanding of how that person really feels about you as a manager and a leader. If you want to take the reverse performance appraisal one step further, sit down and discuss each evaluation with the person who submitted it. This form — and your follow-through — will open the lines of communication between you or your staff like nothing else will.

REVERSE PERFORMANCE APPRAISAL

Manager: _____ Dept.: _____

Employee: _____ Appraisal Period: / / to / /

	Excellent	Good	Improvement Desired	Comments (Be specific)
1. **Quality of Work** Thorough and accurate (requires same from others)	☐	☐	☐	_____
2. **Initiative** Takes action to improve dept.	☐	☐	☐	_____
3. **Availability** There when you need him/her	☐	☐	☐	_____
4. **Planning** Lets you know how/where dept. is going	☐	☐	☐	_____
5. **Delegation Skills** Gives clear instructions	☐	☐	☐	_____
6. **Relationship with Employees** Mutual respect and regard	☐	☐	☐	_____
7. **Decision-Making** Has, or gets, answers; doesn't waffle	☐	☐	☐	_____
8. **Communication Skills** Speaks/writes clearly and directly	☐	☐	☐	_____
9. **Promptness** Starts meetings, appointments, etc. on time	☐	☐	☐	_____
10. **Time Management** Completes work efficiently	☐	☐	☐	_____
11. **Leadership Skills** Inspires dedication and loyalty	☐	☐	☐	_____
12. **Approachability** Open and attentive to your concerns	☐	☐	☐	_____
13. **Training/Development** Helps with your professional growth	☐	☐	☐	_____
14. **Creativity/Problem-Solving** Has good ideas and solutions	☐	☐	☐	_____
15. **Fairness** Does not have favourites	☐	☐	☐	_____

Please write any further specifics, examples, and solutions (as well as general comments) on the back.

Figure 20.2 Reverse performance appraisal

After you have gone through your reverse performance evaluation (and ideally targeted areas for improvement), put all of your completed forms away until your next review in six months. See how the same people rate you on the same issues. Where did you improve? Where have you slipped? Make this exercise a leadership 'checkup' you give yourself on a regular basis. *One word of caution*: Don't use the form unless you are truly open to criticism. If you ignore or resist the constructive feedback you get, you'll only reinforce any negative perceptions your people may have of you.

For our sceptical readers who believe their employees won't be straight with them: try our form just once. We predict you'll be amazed at how honest and constructively critical people can be when given the chance. If you do receive a too-good-to-be-true review, send it back with a note saying, 'Thanks, but nobody's *this* perfect. Surely I need to improve somewhere. Try again.' Doing this will signal to any particularly suspicious people that you really are open to changing and improving, and won't penalize them for being truthful with you. The second time around you'll get all the honest feedback you want. We promise.

Set — and Achieve — Your Goals

The Magic of Goal-Setting

The first step in achieving your goals is to recognize that 'someday' is not a day of the week.
— ED BLISS, *GETTING THINGS DONE*

Here's the truth: the difference between achieving and not achieving is goal-setting. Those who set goals achieve a great deal; those who don't generally achieve little.

Self-improvement does not require that you be dissatisfied with the way you are now, forever focused on some faraway goal. It means enjoying the process as much as the result. There's a special joy in seeing yourself break out of the rut in life, overcome the negative programming you've been stuck with, and blossom in ways you never thought possible. The purpose of life is growth, and positive growth is much easier with a goal-achievement system.

In this way the key purpose of goal-setting is self-knowledge. By finding out what you want, you also find out who you are. Finding out what you want may at first sound easy: you want a new car, you want to go to sleep, you want some sweets, you want to go out on the town. If anything, you may think you'd be better off if you thought a little less about what you want. But knowing what you want on a short-term, day-to-day basis is different from knowing what you want out of life.

The blunt fact is that most people conduct their careers according to other people's expectations. They dutifully enter the career for which they were groomed by their parents and teachers. On the job they do everything they feel is expected of them, but nothing more. For them, work could never be a means of expression or fulfilment or anything more than a means to money and status. That's no way to live, nor is it a way to succeed. To muster the energy and enthusiasm it takes to really succeed in the professional world — and it takes a lot — you must love what you do. Otherwise, it's too much hard work;

and in the final analysis it's inspiration, not hard work, that breeds success.

It's important to keep your career moving in the direction of your greatest enjoyment and satisfaction. Put simply, you must identify the aspects of your job that you like and then expand them. Direct your energy towards that which gives you the biggest thrill. At the same time let go of the boring or anxiety-producing aspects. The key is to make this an ongoing, everyday process. Fortunately, professionals today are freer to engineer their own careers. Organizations are reaching new levels of flexibility and individual accommodation. No two functions need be alike. Your pursuit of professional happiness may lead you to places you never expected to go — you may find that the voice telling you to leave sales and open a bed-and-breakfast was the one you should have listened to all along. Be open to it. You'll never regret it.

But truly taking charge of your own pursuit of happiness through goal-setting is, frankly, scary. In fact, it's so scary that many people purposely busy themselves with the *wants* of life as a means of distracting themselves from facing the *goals* of life. They build careers, raise families, and dutifully go through the motions without ever questioning whether what they are getting is what will really fulfill them. Many fear self-knowledge will show them that fulfilment requires dismantling their present life and constructing a new one. What they don't know is that the people who have done this successfully, painful as it can be, are among the happiest people on earth.

So while setting goals may be scary, it is necessary. Because if you don't have the courage to pursue your own goals, you leave yourself open to the many people who will be only too happy to recruit you to pursue theirs.

THE HOW-TO-DO-ITS

1. Enter into goal-setting
In other words, enter into taking control over your life. Reject

the route that most people take: shuffling down the lifepath of least resistance, resigned to 'making the most of it'. True, life has a momentum of its own — and while you must respect that, chances are you *can* control your life much more than you do now.

After six years in the professional-development business, Jimmy still hadn't bought into the concept of goal-setting — it seemed too contrived. Not until he was on holiday several years ago did he discover the raw power of writing goals on paper. In the middle of his trip, he was getting a little bored. So he pulled out a pen and pad and, sitting by the pool, he asked himself, 'What am I going to do when I get back?' Jimmy had been in business for himself for a couple of years and wanted to expand, so he made a list of some of the things he wanted to accomplish. He let his imagination run wild and wrote down his most ambitious fantasies. ('I would have been embarrassed if anyone else had seen them,' he says.)

But one year later he was no longer embarrassed; he was a believer. Because everything he had scribbled down had happened — and more. Jimmy had doubled the size of his business and started two new ones. He'd tripled his income. He'd written a book. He'd taken on a partner, and his career was skyrocketing. Needless to say, Jimmy has been a compulsive goal-setter ever since.

2. Start by fantasizing

This is the fun part. How often do people take the time actually to think about their own dreams for the future? Most of us are too busy keeping up with the day-to-day treadmill of life.

There are several questions you can ask yourself to get in touch with your fantasies. Some of our favourites are the following: If you could do anything, what would you do? If you could be anyone, who would you be? What would you do if you knew you couldn't fail? What would you do for nothing? Imagine that you are chatting with the person you are going to be in ten years. How does that person look, speak, and think? Does he or she have any advice for you? What were your childhood daydreams? What are your adult daydreams?

Let your imagination soar. This is *your* life and you can make it whatever you want. And don't feel guilty just because this exercise is a lot of fun. As we've said, this is not frivolity! Most people fail to get what they want because they refuse to let themselves think about it. After you do you will be far more qualified to commit your goals to paper and start yourself on your way to achieving what you really want in life.

3. Set up a written goal-setting system

This simple process is a giant step towards realizing your goals. It's been said that the difference between a 'wish' and a 'goal' is that a goal is written down. Believe it. Putting your goals on paper allows you literally to see them, which makes them much easier to rework, focus, prioritize, and *use*.

Figure 21.1 shows a master goal-setting sheet that will help you commit your goals to paper. Take a look at it now, and see that we've presented eight categories in which to set your goals: physical, relationships/family, financial, career, service, self-development, social, and spiritual. In the rest of this chapter we will show you how to use this system to make goal-setting work for you. The most important thing to remember is to *make your goals your own*. Change or add to our categories if you wish. Likewise, the examples we list under each category are meant only to trigger your own goals — don't feel that you have to use them.

4. Turn your goals into deadlines

Now you're ready to fill out your master goal-setting sheet. The trick is to break your long-term goals into short-term ones and assign them deadlines. Deadlines have a magical way of producing results, so give yourself lots of them. The reason is simple: a five- or even one-year goal is very hard to work with. For instance, if your goal is to invest $30 000 within five years, it's easy to put it off. Why not? You've got lots of time. But by breaking it down into a monthly or even a weekly goal, you have something tangible to work with. You know that you want to invest $6000 by this time next year, which means $500 a month or $250 every pay day. Now that's the way to make things happen.

It's essential that these short-term goals and deadlines be written down on your master goal-setting sheet. We suggest setting two to six goals in each category. That way you have

MASTER GOAL-SETTING SHEET
Date: _____

PHYSICAL
10 years: _____

5 years: _____

1 year: *Examples:*

    Weigh _____ lbs. by _____ (lose/gain _____ lbs. per month).

    Run _____ miles _____ in minutes by _____ .

    Do _____ sit-ups by _____ .

    Get a physical from Dr. _____ by _____ .

RELATIONSHIPS/FAMILY
10 years: _____

5 years: _____

1 year: *Examples:*

    Date one new person per _____ .

    Get pregnant by _____ .

    Have _____ family vacations/weekends (where? when?).

    Remember, these are examples. You probably should not do all three.

FINANCIAL
10 years: _____

5 years: _____

1 year: *Examples:*

    Get a _____ % raise by _____ .

    Save _____ by _____ (_____ per week).

    Buy _____ properties.

    Buy _____ government stock.

CAREER
10 years: _____

5 years: _____

1 year: *Examples:*

    Get a promotion to __(position)__ by _____ .

    Employ _____ people by _____ (specify positions).

    Get a new job by _____ .

      Research prospective companies by _____ .

    Start my business by _____ .

      Write business plan by _____ .

      Arrange financing by _____ .

      Lease space by, _____ etc.

Figure 21.1   Master goal-setting sheet

SERVICE

10 years: _____

5 years: _____

1 year: *Examples:*

        Join _____ by _____ .

        Arrange to do volunteer work

        at _____ by _____ .

        Donate _____ to _____ by _____ .

        Write article about _____ and submit it

        to _____ by _____ .

SELF-DEVELOPMENT

10 years: _____

5 years: _____

1 year: *Examples:*

        Read _____ books (_____ career books; _____ novels).

        Attend _____ seminars/retreats/conferences.

        Listen to _____ audiocassette programmes.

        View _____ videocassette programmes.

        Learn _____ skills/procedures.

        Skydive at least once by _____ .

SOCIAL

10 years: _____

5 years: _____

1 year: *Examples:*

        Have _____ parties/dinners.

        Try _____ new restaurants.

        See _____ films.

        Attend _____ plays.

        Attend _____ concerts.

        Call or write to an old friend every _____ .

SPIRITUAL

10 years: _____

5 years: _____

1 year: *Examples:*

        Attend church every_____ .

        Try _____ new churches/synagogues/meetings.

        Meditate _____ times per week.

Figure 21.1 (cont.)

something to aim for, but it doesn't become overwhelmingly complicated. This divide-and-conquer approach gives you the small, immediate victories that keep your momentum going.

5. Make them specific and measurable

Let's say your one-year goal is to become 'more visible' in your company. What does that really mean? What committees or special projects will you have to volunteer for? What initiatives can you spearhead (and how can you publicize them)? What honours can you aim for? How many articles should you have published in the company newsletter? When? The problem (and opportunity!) is that any combination of a hundred things can add up to 'visibility'. Only when you specify and quantify what *you* mean by visibility can you get on the road to achieving it.

6. Make them realistic and compatible

Unfortunately, deciding what is realistic is tough. Is it realistic to set the goal of becoming a millionaire in five years? Of living in Tahiti? Of achieving oneness with the universe? Only you can decide what is realistic for you. One thing is certain, however: it's better to set your goals too high than too low. Breaking down your goals into short-term deadlines is the best way we know to judge if you're reaching too far. Consider: if you want to have read sixty fiction classics in five years, you know that you ought to be reading one book per month, and you have to get through about a fourth of *War and Peace* this week — good luck! Upon seeing that, you may decide to revise your goal.

7. Review your goals monthly (at least)

We suggest you do a special goal-review exercise once a month (we usually budget an hour on a Sunday night — it's become a welcome ritual). At this goal-setting session pull out your master goal-setting sheet and put each goal to the 'Four Rs' test. Scrutinize them in terms of *revising* (' I still want to achieve this goal, but not quite the way I had planned'); *removing* ('I'm no longer interested in reaching this goal; I think I'll forget it'); *rescheduling* ('I still want to do this, but I haven't made time for it yet — I'll set a new, more realistic deadline'), and *rewarding* ('I did it! Time to buy a bar of chocolate').

Your monthly goal-setting session is the time to be honest about which goals you're really committed to and which ones are only paper dreams. Which ones have you ignored? Which are you completely avoiding? It's OK to change and abandon goals — get rid of them and feel good about it! Then recommit to the ones you are dead serious about, and feel good about that, too. You're in control of your life.

Making adjustments is a natural result of focusing on what is important to you. Make changes freely, and if your goal-setting sheet gets too messy, take a few minutes to write a new one. Remember, the direction you got from setting goals is just as important as the achievements themselves. True goal-setting supports your personal evolution, it doesn't tie you to some immutable plan. By the way, it's a good idea to keep your monthly goal-setting sheets (a three-ring binder is perfect for organizing them). They make a fascinating record of your feelings and ambitions throughout your life.

8. Keep your goals central in your life

While a monthly review is essential, a quick daily review also is helpful. One way to do this is to carry your latest goal-setting sheet update (or a copy) folded in your diary so you can look over it whenever you have a few minutes. Or condense your work-related goals into five or six sentences and hang them on the wall in your office, or tape them to the front of a drawer in your desk. We're not advocating becoming a slave to your goals. But by keeping your attention focused on them, you will minimize the chances of getting caught up in trivia or wasting time on accomplishments that aren't really important to you.

9. Persist and prevail

Just because you are free to change your goals doesn't mean you should. The magic word for achieving anything is *persistence*. How many goals have you failed to reach when you wouldn't give up? Probably very few. People who reach their goals find ways to circumvent the roadblocks and wrong turns. Rule of thumb: abandon goals only if they've lost meaning for you — never because they're too tough or you've had a setback.

We're reminded of what President Coolidge said: 'Nothing in the world can take the place of persistence. Talent will not; nothing is more common than unsuccessful people with talent. Genius will not; unrewarded genius is almost a proverb. Education will not; the world is full of educated derelicts. Persistence and determination alone are omnipotent.'

10. Use goal-setting to manage

Just as goals give your career new energy and direction, they can do the same for any people you may supervise. Here's how the system works: get all staff who report to you to set at least three goals for the next three months. At the end of the three months, meet with them and see how they did. If the goal-setting system was done properly (and in a moment we'll show you how to ensure that it is), it will be very clear to both you and your employees how well they are progressing.

Another way to use goal-setting as a management tool is to encourage two or more people to share a three-month goal. that way they're motivated to support each other; it's not only more fun, it's more productive. Today's most successful managers are the ones skilled at building teams, and shared goals are a good way to do it.

In Figure 21.2 we've adapted a form we use at CareerTrack to make this process as easy and effective as possible Notice that writing each goal on this form is a four-step process. It's a very important process, and you must be diligent as a teacher/coach to make sure every step is done correctly. But beware: goal-setting is, strangely enough, not a natural process for most people, and you may be surprised at how strongly they resist it. Let's look at the four steps on the form one by one:

Step A is actually to state the goal. As we know, a goal must be specific and measurable. That means 'reorganize the department library so more people use it' would not be acceptable. It would have to be rewritten to say, for instance, 'increase usage of the department library by 15 per cent'. Likewise, 'improve relations with our distributors' would have to be changed to something like 'launch a monthly newsletter to our distributors'. Don't forget, you're looking for action, not good intentions.

Step B is to state the strategies and activities your employee will use to achieve his or her goal. For the library example above, the strategies and activities might be 'to 1   reorganize the library using the Dewey decimal system; 2   publicize a 'book and tape of the week' in the department newsletter; 3   meet individually with all managers to assess their needs and update them on what's available; 4   get a table and chairs to make it more comfortable to browse and work in the library', and so on. Again, you're looking for specifics.

Step C is to agree on the measurement standards. This is a crucial step where you and your employee decide on how you are going to know if the goal was achieved. The library example may seem fairly easy: either usage went up 15 per cent or it didn't. But how will you know? Will you base the figure on how many books and tapes were checked out, or on a before-and-after usage survey of the people in the department, or on how many people walk in and out of the library every day? You and your employee must agree *in advance* on what the measurement standards are.

Step D is the grand finale. This is filled out at the end of three months. As we've said, if you have done an adequate job of defining goals, activities, and measurement standards, the result will be self-evident.

You're not finished yet, though. The purpose of this goal-setting system is to extract all the subjectivity out of how you measure your people's contributions. But, alas, we can never really do that. After the goal-setting system is complete, you have to make judgements and draw conclusions from what you've found. For instance, what if your employee created an 11 per cent increase in library usage instead of 15 per cent? Is that a failure? Well, that's for you to decide, and you can base your decision on many factors: is momentum for the library growing; does your employee still seem enthused; does the increased usage seem to have increased the productivity, motivation, etc. of the people in the department? This is where quantification no longer works, and you and your employee have to use good judgement.

You'll also notice a place for signatures and some open-ended comments at the end of the form. The manager's pre-quarter comments are usually not much more than a 'you-can-do-it' pep talk. The signatures simply get and record commitment (ever

Name _____ Quarter _____ Year _____
MY GOALS _____ THROUGH _____
Here's your chance to declare your three major professional goals
for the next quarter. These goals should be the ones you feel
most 'passionate' about — the ones you can commit yourself
to 100 per cent. If you don't have a burning desire to achieve
them, you probably won't. Also, your goals should be compatible
with (company or department)'s needs and goals — make sure that they
sufficiently overlap with your job responsibilities.
     State your goals of the *specific* and *realistic* results you want.
State your *strategies and activities* in terms of how you will
measure and *verify* your results. Please note: specific goals can
be quantified. If you can't associate a number with a goal, it's
probably not specific enough. To that end, avoid all vague,
ambiguous language. After you complete your goal-setting sheet,
discuss it with your manager and get a mutual agreement. At
the end of the quarter, fill in your *results* in terms of whether
your goals were achieved.
     Good advice: keep your goal-sheet in a location where you
will look at it every day. Review your progress every day and
be prepared to report it at the weekly meeting.
1. A. Major Goal 1 _____

   _____
   _____

   B. Strategies and Activities _____
   _____
   _____

   C. Measurement Standards _____
   _____
   D. Results _____
   _____
2. A. Major Goal 2 _____
   _____
   _____

   B. Strategies and Activities _____
   _____
   _____

   C. Measurement Standards _____
   _____
   D. Results _____
   _____

Figure 21.2   Goal-setting form

3. A. Major Goal 3 _____

_____

_____

_____

B. Strategies and Activities _____

_____

_____

_____

C. Measurement Standards _____

_____

D. Results _____

_____

Manager's Pre-Quarter Comments _____

_____

_____

I agree that these goals are realistic, measurable, **compatible**, and verifiable:

Your Signature _____ Date _____

Manager's Signature _____ Date _____

****

Your Post-Quarter Comments _____

_____

_____

_____

Manager's Post-Quarter Comments _____

_____

_____

_____

_____

Figure 21.2 (Contd.)

notice how seriously people regard documents they have to sign?). The post-quarter comments are the most important. They record your *interpretation* of what was achieved, including, for instance, what mitigating factors had an impact, any suggested redirection for future goals, the value in retrospect of the goal, and so forth.

A clever side benefit of the three-month goal-setting system is that it empowers your staff to take charge of their own productivity and achievements. They have a big hand in setting their own goals (and you'll notice that people will voluntarily take on bigger challenges than you would have dared to 'assign' them); they take pride in ownership in achieving them on schedule; and, best of all, they see their results with their own eyes. When people fail to reach their goals quarter after quarter, they realize they're not making it. You may find that they come to you for a transfer (lateral or even downward). It's happened to us several times, and every one of these people is now productive and happy in his or her new position. Sometimes they'll even resign, which may be the best of all solutions when an employee is consistently not making it.

11. Ask yourself, 'Why do I want this?'

As we mentioned at the beginning of this chapter, the *process* of goal-setting is as important as the result. A major misconception about goals is that once they are set they must be achieved. This attitude is not only misguided, it is destructive and the source of a lot of anxiety and low self-esteem. As yoga master Swami Satchidananda told an audience recently, 'Want nothing and you will have everything.' He explained, 'If you want something, all you will end up with is something. If you want nothing, you will end up with everything. Nothing and everything look alike.'

Swami, himself a great achiever, was probably overstating his case just a bit. But he was not talking nonsense. On the contrary, for those who are writing and reading books of advice, Swami had some of the best advice around.

'No way,' you say. 'There are 10 000 things I want. Furthermore, I want to continue to want them and someday to have them.'

So often we dedicate ourselves to the pursuit of a goal, thinking that once we achieve it we will have it made. We deny ourselves, put everything else in abeyance, and set out on a single-minded quest for achievement. We think, 'If I work hard and sacrifice now, later things will be rosy'. But with that kind of attitude things will never be rosy. How many times have you achieved a major goal — getting into a certain university, entering a relationship, buying a new toy, getting a new job — only to find that it wasn't quite what you had expected and didn't necessarily make you any happier? The process of living for anticipated fulfilment can go on indefinitely, with fulfilment always just out of reach. It's an easy trap to fall into.

12. Start this second

The system we've laid out in this chapter is easily the most powerful you will find in the entire book. We say this because goal-settting is what activates the rest of the things in the book. Goal-setting transforms you from being a thinker and contemplator to being a doer and achiever. Don't just leave this chapter with good intentions about goal-setting. And don't wait until next Sunday night, don't wait until your birthday, and please don't wait until New Year's Day to get started. *Do something now*. Trust us. Spend one hour fantasizing and filling out the questions in Figure 21.2, and we guarantee that you'll be more optimistic, motivated, and in control of your life than you've been in a long time.

Gain Visibility and Get Noticed

Be Seen, Get Known, Move Ahead

Make the most of your best.
— DOROTHY SARNOFF

Business is not a subtle profession. In fact, when it comes to standing out and getting noticed, there are no subtle professions. To achieve real success, it's not enough to be good at what you do; you must be *seen* being good at what you do.

The goal is not celebrity — it is opportunity. When you're visible, your name comes up more often. Think about it: when your manager is looking for someone to head a coveted project, who comes to mind, the good low-visibility candidate or the good high-visibility candidate? Both may be capable, yet only one is remembered. When you're getting the choice assignments, can promotions and salary increases be far behind? Besides, having your successes acknowledged and seen now and then feels wonderful.

Visibility draws you to the people whom you need and who need you. For instance, it is customary for scientists to publish their findings quickly. They do this for three reasons: to help people who are struggling with the same problems; to get credit; and to alert other scientists who might have the next key in their ongoing puzzle. The synergy of 'publishing quickly' can occur in any profession, linking people together and enabling them to 'plus' one another's work.

One caveat: visibility leverages substance — it does not replace it. The point of visibility is to get people's attention. After that, you've got to deliver on what you promised and *earn* their respect. In other words, looking like a million bucks does not mean you'll make a million bucks. To achieve real success you're also going to need some of the other professional attributes, such as brains and guts.

Closely tied to the process of gaining visibility is the skill of networking. Networking connects you with people, keeps your profile high, and gives you a 'face' out there. It's so important, in fact, that we've given networking its own chapter, Success Shortcut 25.

THE HOW-TO-DO-ITS

1. Think of yourself as a product

This is not meant to be dehumanizing; it simply makes understanding the process of gaining visibility a whole lot easier. The basics of advertising and marketing a product are: gain attention, get someone to 'try' you, then deliver on your promise so they'll use you again. There's really nothing more to gaining visibility — and success — in your organization and profession. Keep this marketing model in mind as you consider the following ideas.

2. Look the part

Like a product, you must visually satisfy the 'buyer's' expectation. Appearance counts, and don't underestimate how much. Furthermore, there's no one right way to dress. If you're a banker, the look is obviously different from if you're an art director or a farmer. When you look like you're at the top of your profession people will assume you are, and this will colour the rest of what they learn about you to support that predisposition.

In the past few years there has been a lot of talk on the subject of how to dress as a professional. If you feel you need help in this area, by all means read one of the many books on the subject (see our Recommended Resources on page 257). Personal appearance is not an incidental; no matter what your profession, you'll have a better chance of success if you dress and present yourself in a manner considered appropriate. Not taking your appearance seriously can damage you enormously, especially if you are entering a profession that requires adherence to traditional, conservative styles. The following true story about two friends of Jimmy's illustrates just how much it can hurt.

Tom and Bill were good friends who had just graduated from Princeton with degrees in accounting. Both were above-average students and well-liked. Tom was outgoing and athletic, and always took time to look good. Bill, though also outgoing, was a bit overweight and paid less attention to his appearance. After graduation, both Tom and Bill interviewed with all the big eight accounting firms. Tom received several job offers (and accepted one), while Bill got nothing but rejections. After one of his unsuccessful interviews, Bill's interviewer explained why. The man said, 'Bill, we have no doubt that you could do a good job, but in all honesty we can't hire you, because we don't feel you would present the right image to our clients'.

Bill got the message and immediately went on a self-improvement kick. He got a haircut, lost some weight, and bought a couple of new suits. This is when things went from bad to worse. He scheduled a second round of interviews, this time with a number of private accounting firms, but still was not able to obtain a position. When he received his final letter of rejection, he called the personnel director at a company where he thought he had made a strong impression and asked why he had not been employed. The interviewer answered that the company had considered Bill carefully, but could not figure out why none of the big eight firms had hired him. They assumed the other firms had discovered something negative about Bill that they had overlooked, and they were reluctant to take any chances.

A bad personal appearance may not hurt you as much as it hurt Bill, but it will most definitely have a negative impact. Make sure you look the part you want to play.

So what *is* the appropriate image for an up-and-coming achiever like yourself? That depends, for one thing, on the field you are in. For example, lawyers, accountants, and business executives usually wear conventional business suits. This standard is loosening in some circles, but it is still safe and accepted. Doctors and dentists wear white coats. Field engineers wear very expensive yet casual outdoor clothes. Architects and commercial artists must show a little flair (otherwise no one will think they have any talent). And university professors can still get away with affecting a disdain for appearance by holding out for the rumpled look.

It will help you if, within the context of a look that is appropriate, you show a little flair. Try to develop a style that is original and distinctive, then stick with it. There are numerous elements to work with — for example, a certain colour, fabric, or tailoring style. When people can begin to identify you by a certain 'look', you will have gone a long way towards achieving professional visibility.

3. Stay late

Very often you'll find an organization's successful employees working after hours. The first advantage to working late is that it's a great time to get things done — there are fewer distractions. Second, it's an opportunity for you to get tied in with top achievers in your company, and vice versa (the camaraderie after hours can be great fun). Third, you're gaining visibility with upper management, which — trust us — makes it a point to know who's putting in extra hours. Working longer days demonstrates commitment, and it's impossible to ignore. We're not advocating workaholism or martyrdom. It's just that success rarely happens in forty hours a week, and those who have achieved it know it.

4. Join up

Being active in your professional associations is a good way to gain visibility with the key people in your industry. At company or industry meetings you'll be able to make valuable contacts, keep abreast of what's happening in your field, and just 'get around'. And don't just join — participate! Volunteer for committee assignments, even run for elective offices (generally nobody wants them). These positions will vastly enhance your visibility throughout your profession.

5. 'Propose' to your boss

Upper management loves new ideas on how to increase profits, cut costs, and improve the working environment. When you have an insight on how to achieve one of these goals, write it up and get it to the decision-makers in the company. Submit your proposal to your immediate superior. If he or she is not empowered to make the final decision, make sure it is passed on to his or her boss, *with your name on it.* (If you have a boss who insists on taking credit for your ideas, find a new boss, even if that means finding a new company.)

In our company, every new employee is given a form titled 'My ideas on how to do something better at CareerTrack' (a sample appears in Figure 22.1), and asked to copy and use it often. When employees have ideas to bounce off management, they fill out this form and submit it to their supervisors, who comment on the ideas and then route the forms directly to their own managers.

While top management can't always drop everything to listen to a verbal presentation, this form ensures that every person eventually will be heard. It also brings a certain discipline to the suggestion process by forcing people to consider some key questions, such as exactly how much time and money the idea will save (or generate), and whether the company can afford to implement it. Best of all, if a good idea is submitted, the person who had it always gets the credit. It's a form that gets attention and works.

6. Become a committed card sender

Are there people whose attention you have a hard time getting? People in this category might include upper managers, company stars, or industry heavyweights. A simple card can get through when nothing else can. It might be a congratulatory card (for a promotion or a great speech), a thank-you card (for approving your attendance at a seminar), even a simple Christmas card. A few people in our company send us cards on special occasions. It's not at all expected, and we think no less of those who don't do it. Yet we're only human, and the people who get our attention are more likely to be remembered.

7. Specialize. Specialize. Specialize

Every product has its niche. What's yours? Just as doctors specialize in paediatrics or surgery, managers can specialize in budgeting or personnel problems, and clerical people can specialize in words or numbers. Stay an all-rounder, but find one thing to be *the best* at. Then people will seek you out.

You can specialize, not just in the type of work you do but in how you do it. A consultant we use says his goal is to be the easiest consultant for a company to work with. He

'MY IDEAS ON HOW TO DO SOMETHING BETTER AT...'

Date submitted _____

By _____

Department _____

The Problem/Opportunity: _____

_____

_____

My Proposed New Way: _____

_____

_____

Benefits to Organization: _____

_____

_____

The Potential Hang-ups: _____

_____

_____

Estimated Time and Money Savings: _____

Estimated Costs to Implement: _____

Who Should Implement This Idea: _____

Supervisor's Comments: _____

_____

_____

And the Final Decision Is... _____

_____

_____

Figure 22.1   'My ideas on how to do something better' form

may not be the cheapest or the most experienced, but he *is* the easiest to work with. It's an intriguing, appealing market position, one he promotes *and delivers on*.

8. Get a gimmick

Irving R. Levine, one of American television's most visible reporters, is known for his bow ties. He has worn them consistently over the years, when they're in style and when they're not. They've become a trademark that people notice and remember. President Reagan brings jelly beans to Cabinet meetings. A manager we know always includes a joke in his company's weekly newsletter. It's usually a bad joke, but people look forward to it and laugh anyway. Think about it: do you have an eccentricity that you've been swallowing so you could 'fit in'? If it's harmless and memorable, consider showing it off. It not only feels better (it's wonderful to be able to express your true self at work), but it helps raise your profile.

9. Become part of someone else's routine

That 'someone' being the person from whom you're trying to get recognition (for instance, your boss). A good way to do this is by submitting a weekly accomplishment sheet complete with updates on current projects, problems/solutions, and new ideas. By getting the person above you to expect and look forward to your weekly report, you'll keep your visibility high. The key to this is *consistency*. Don't do it only when the mood strikes you, but regularly, week after week.

10. Take the credit

Ask yourself this question: 'What have I accomplished today that can help other people do their jobs better?' For example, did you prepare a report for your sales force that your accounting department might find useful? Then send them a copy, with your compliments. You'll not only be helping them, you'll also be helping yourself by raising your visibility with them. When you receive praise, accept it graciously (and give it freely — people rarely get enough). And never take credit, no matter how little, for something you did not do.

11. Be the presenter

Public speaking is probably the one skill that builds visibility faster than any other. Has your company, group, or department come up with a new idea, system, or solution that others ought to know about? What association, department, or group would benefit from hearing about it? Volunteer to present it! It's a great way to establish yourself as an authority (speakers are generally associated with the ideas they present, whether or not they came up with them). If you think you need to polish your public speaking skills or overcome a phobia about speaking in front of others, there is help. (See Success Shortcut 17.)

12. Raise your hand for the big ones

In other words, volunteer for high-visibility assignments. For example, write your department's memos, reports, and news-letters (don't just be the presenter, be the writer; see Success Shortcut 15). Other possibilities are leading discussion groups, championing projects that give you the opportunity to interact with large numbers of people (especially those at the top), organizing the Christmas party — anything that puts you in the limelight in your company. Look around: there are visibility vacuums all around your company. Sign up to fill them.

One of the best ways to volunteer for high-visibility assign-ments is to invite yourself to high-visibility meetings. Here's an example: when Jeff owned his first company, a small advertis-ing agency in Boulder, he had a client, Vicki, for whom he did a lot of work month after month. Vicki's company was owned by a huge corporation. One day John, the president of this parent organization, called Jeff to say, 'Jeff, I've been watching the work you've been doing for our division and I like it. I wonder if you'd be interested in meeting with me to talk about doing some work for us?' Jeff was thrilled. They made an appointment, and without even putting down the phone, Jeff called Vicki to tell her the good news. She congratulated him and wished him the best.

But Vicki, a very smart woman, went one step further. She immediately wrote John a note saying, 'You know, John, Jeff and I have been working together very effectively for quite a while now. I know how he works; we communicate well. Would it be helpful if I sat in on your first meeting just to facilitate the communication?' What a great idea! Of course John agreed.

Vicki attended John and Jeff's first meeting and played quite a valuable role. She subsequently went to every meeting they had for the next two years and always contributed a lot. As we said, Vicki is clever. She knew that John and Jeff probably wouldn't think to invite her to their meeting; that's just how the world works. But she also knew that she truly had something to offer. So she took the initiative to invite herself, and in the process she gained enormously valuable visibility with someone who was very important to her career. Normally Vicki perhaps would have seen John at the Christmas party, and he probably wouldn't have known her name. But after that first meeting, he knew her name — and he also knew what a capable woman she was.

Incidentally, a couple of years later, when John sold Vicki's division and most of the people were laid off, Vicki was invited to join the parent company. Vicki played it just right by not waiting to be included in those meetings. And, again, the key is that she wasn't muscling in just for the sake of visibility. She really *did* have a lot to offer.

Attend Seminars and Get Ahead

Invest in Yourself

It's no accident that the world's leading technology company, IBM, spends $500 million per year in training, educating, and re-educating its employees.
— PAUL HAWKEN, *THE NEXT ECONOMY*

Smart professionals know that education doesn't end after college. In order to stay on top of your career — and out in front of your competition — you have to make learning an ongoing, lifelong process.

Seminars (short-term courses ranging from a half-day to a week in length) are the preferred means of continuing education for most professionals. Why? Because they're short, practical, and up-to-the-minute.

Unlike college, seminars don't require a large time and money commitment. And unlike reading books and journals, attending seminars *immerses* you in the information and skills you need. In many cases you practise your new skills with special exercises. The intense, high-energy environment of a typical business seminar not only helps you learn, it also can be a lot of fun. The shot-in-the-arm you get will leave you as fired-up as you are smarter.

At a seminar you get a good perspective on how you're doing in your own career. Nothing beats a day away from your desk for a close examination of your role in your company, the people with whom you work, and your personal goals and how well you're achieving them. Also, you'll meet other people who are in the same boat as you. Ever wonder how other people do it? Ever need a little reassurance you're doing it the 'right' way? Making contacts is one of the best hidden benefits of seminars. Where better to meet people just like you, who are successful and growing? Just think: at your next seminar you may find a new customer or supplier — even a new job.

But let's face it, sometimes the idea of going to a

seminar can be a bit of a turnoff — especially if it's on a subject like assertiveness training or image building. 'What kind of people need to go to that?' you may ask yourself. 'What kind of losers am I going to be associated with?'

On the contrary, if you've ever gone to a seminar, you've probably found yourself among some of the top people in your field. After all, these are the people who are taking the time to learn new ideas, new solutions to old problems, and new approaches to achieving their goals. It's no wonder they're successful.

Whether you're interested in a technical topic like marketing or finance, or a personal-growth topic like stress management or time management, there is a seminar available to meet your needs. Here's how we recommend you get the most out of your next seminar.

THE HOW-TO-DO-ITS

1. Make sure it's proven

Been to a good seminar lately? Usually, it's a hit-or-miss proposition, unless you check it out in advance. How? By asking the sponsor for the names and phone numbers of past attendees. If you invest fifteen minutes to call these people, you may well save yourself from wasting a lot more time on a poor programme. Ask your references if the seminar met their expectations, what they got out of it, and if they are using what they learned. If you like what you hear, sign up and go. (If, in order to protect its customers' privacy, the sponsor refuses to give out phone numbers, ask for copies of past evaluations, and make sure a full money-market guarantee is offered.)

2. Ask to go

Most organizations pay for their employees to attend seminars (after all, it's an investment for both). However, getting time off and permission to spend some of your organization's training budget on a seminar isn't always an easy matter. A simple verbal request is sometimes all it takes, but a written request is better. Consider writing a memo to your boss and/or training director, outlining the feature of the seminar. If you have some literature on the seminar, include it, highlight the parts that show how you — and the company — will benefit. That way your boss and training director can see immediately what's in it for them if they pay your way.

3. Remember your goals

Why did you decide to register for the seminar? What do you expect to gain? Take a minute to think about your goals, then clarify them by writing them down. Be sure to include any problems you're having or questions you need answered. Look over your goal sheet again every morning of the programme; it will help you get in the right frame of mind for obtaining what you want from the seminar.

4. Think ahead

Arrive early to allow time to register, meet a few people, get a good seat, and settle in. If you're driving to the seminar, make sure you know exactly where you're going (walking in late and stressful is no way to begin a seminar). Also, plan for your comfort. Have an ample supply of tissues, mints, writing paper, and anything else you need. And bring a sweater or jacket — the temperature fluctuates in most hotel or conference centre meeting rooms. After all, you won't learn much if you're shivering to death.

5. Meet and mingle

As we've said, a seminar is an excellent opportunity to expand your network of contacts. Sit next to someone you don't know, even if you've come with a group. Mingle during the breaks. Exchange business cards. Every participant has a specific area of expertise; find out what it is instead of chatting about the weather. Remember the goal sheet in point three? Let us suggest that one of your goals be to meet at least one person you intend to see again on a business or social basis. Don't forget business cards!

6. Get involved with the action

Ask questions. Make contributions. Talk to the trainer during breaks. Participate wholeheartedly in the exercises. This is the real reason to attend a seminar. If you had just wanted information, you could have listened to a tape programme. The beauty of a seminar is that you can *participate* in your learning. Therefore, consider the meeting room to be a 'mental gymnasium', where it's OK to run, fall down, and get up again. You'll benefit much more by participating in the game than by sitting on the sidelines. But, please, don't overdo it. There's a fine line between participating and being a pest. Be careful not to dominate the discussion with *too much* participation.

7. 'Work' the seminar

Why let even one good idea get away? Taking notes will help you concentrate and organize your thoughts. Plus, notes allow you to take a 'refresher' any time in the future. Be careful that you don't fall into the rut of writing down just what the trainer is saying. Instead, write down *what you're going to do* with what the trainer is saying.

One of our favourite speakers, Mike Vance, once presented a seminar to an audience that included J. Willard Marriott, founder and chairman of the incredibly successful Marriott hotel chain. Naturally Mike kept his eye on his celebrity seminar participant, and soon he noticed that Mr. Marriott was taking notes with both hands — he had a red pen in his right hand and a blue pen in his left. At the time, Mr. Marriott was in his eighties and one of the most revered men in American business, so Mike respected the man's right to do whatever he wanted. Yet, Mike was dying of curiosity.

Finally his curiosity got the better of him, so he stopped the show in mid-sentence, approached the wise old man, and said, 'Excuse me, Mr. Marriott, I couldn't help but notice that you write with both hands. Would you mind telling me why?'

J. Willard Marriott looked up and said, 'It's simple. With my left hand I'm writing down what you are saying, and with my right hand I'm writing down what I'm going to do about it.'

With all due respect to Mr. Marriott, we suggest that you avoid writing what the speaker is saying. The only thing that really matters is what you are going to do about it. Remember

— and it bears repeating — 'It's not what you know that counts, but what you do with what you know'.

So when you go to a seminar or conference, *work it*. Push yourself constantly to think, 'How can I use that information in my job?' Also, look for the one 'big idea' that alone will make the seminar worthwhile. (Rule of thumb: the seminar should have a payback in terms of savings or profits of five times the tuition fee.) The ideas will be there, it's up to you to find them.

8. Relate what you learn to yourself

For instance, if the trainer is talking about sales techniques and you're in sales, think about how you can use the information to be more persuasive with your boss and associates, and even with your spouse and children. In other words, don't settle for 'abstract' knowledge. Continually ask yourself, 'How can I use this information in *my* job? In *my* life?' With your goals, problems, and circumstances foremost in your mind, that shouldn't be too hard.

9. Invest in reinforcement

At many seminars and conventions you can buy audiotapes of the actual sessions, or books and tapes on related topics. These products allow you to 'own' the information in a new way. Learning research shows that two weeks after exposure to any given material, most people have forgotten about 90 per cent of it. The best way to fight this tendency is repetitive learning. You'll not only learn better by hearing or reading the information a second and third time, you'll also pick up new ideas you missed the first time around.

10. Don't call the office

There will always be a problem that 'only you can handle', and in most cases, it *can* wait. Give your associates the seminar location and programme title — in the event of an emergency, you can be paged. Go in relaxed and you'll come out refreshed, inspired, and recharged. Forget about what's happening at the office — unless you have telepathic powers, you can't do much about it anyway. This is your time. Get all you can out of it and enjoy yourself.

11. Commit to act

Spend some time the evening of each seminar day to go over your notes and write down the specific things you intend to start doing differently or better. Use this system for your action plan: write down the new action as simply, specifically, and measurably as you can. (Instead of writing, 'improve communications with my staff', quantify your action by writing, for instance, 'start having a Monday morning staff briefing'.) Then write the date the idea will be implemented, and who will be the 'champion' — either you or a delegate. You'll never be more inspired with new ideas than you are at your evening action session. Don't allow yourself to put away your good ideas with your notes.

12. Send a thank-you letter

If your manager or company sent you to the seminar, thank them (the shock will kill them). Include in your memo a *brief* report based on your action plan, stating what you intend to do or change as a result of this training. Even if you paid your own way, send the report. It will show how committed you are to your own professional growth. Figure 23.1 shows an outline for a 'Dear Boss' letter that you can use to get a good start on your own.

Dear Boss,
    Thanks for approving my attendance at the
_____ seminar. I learned a lot! Here
are some of the highlights:

1. _____

_____

2. _____

_____

3. _____

_____

    I think that the department/company could benefit
from what I learned. Here are some suggestions for
you to consider:

1. _____

_____

2. _____

_____

3. _____

_____

    Again, thanks for the opportunity to attend this
programme. I believe it was a worthwhile investment
— both for me and for the company. I'm already
putting it to use.

                            Sincerely,

                            _____

Figure 23.1   An example of a 'Dear Boss' letter

Learn
with
Audio-
cassettes

Get Ahead with Cassettes

Learning, improving, growing ... you can do it
with cassettes!
— JOEL H. WELDON, *WINNING WITH CASSETTES*

A revolution is happening in the way adults learn. We're talking about the recent explosion in the popularity of spoken-word audiotape programmes.

It's not hard to figure out why. Cassettes present clear, bottom-line benefits in learning. First, the technology is there. In the past few years cassette machines have dropped in price, size, and weight, while increasing quality. The result is that most people have a cassette player today — if not two or three.

Second, cassettes maximize the use of 'mental down-time' in your day. Unlike reading books, listening to cassettes can take place while you're doing other things, such as getting dressed, cooking, exercising — and especially while commuting (whether with your car stereo, or with your Walkman if you take the train, bus, or walk). So join the rush-hour revolution! Turn your commuting time into a way to gain new skills, keep current in your position, and get a regular dose of motivation. Another reward is that you'll be entertained in a way few radio stations can match.

Also, cassettes are generally condensed from full-length books. That means you get only the most important ideas. And remember, according to the 80/20 rule, 80 per cent of a book's value is found in 20 per cent of its pages. Plus, you can easily relisten to cassettes several times. Repetition is a tried-and-true principle for increasing the long-term retention of ideas. In other words, cassettes are an extremely *efficient* way to learn.

There's a more subtle benefit to cassette learning, too. In most cases, the author of the material is presenting it personally. That means you get all the inflection, strength, and colour of the message, 'right from the horse's mouth'.

Cassette learning is easy to integrate into your life. In fact, we boldly predict that it will proliferate and become the preferred way of learning in the near future. The following ideas will help you get ahead with cassettes.

THE HOW-TO-DO-ITS

1. Strategically position tape players and tapes

The best way to integrate tape learning into your lifestyle is to plant tapes and playback machines in all the places where you perform routine activities. That way, when you're ready to learn, all you have to do is push 'play'. Exactly *where* should you position tape players? In your car, office, kitchen, bathroom, bedroom — everywhere you spend large blocks of time. (Don't forget to put one in your briefcase and another in your exercise bag — cassettes are great for stationary bicycles.) With the low cost of a portable machine, you can probably afford several. You can even have different programmes going in a couple of places at once so you won't have to transport tapes.

2. Invest in a fast-play tape machine

Because of computer-chip technology, you can now experience spoken-word cassettes in half the time — *and* increase your comprehension in the process. With variable-speed tape recorders, the speaker talks faster without raising the voice pitch. Speed listening is not only faster, it's more efficient because your mind doesn't have the chance to wander (you can comprehend up to 450 words a minute, yet most people talk at only 125 wpm). Studies show that retention actually goes up when you listen at faster speeds. Most speed-listening machines allow you to control the playback pace so you can listen from normal up to two times the original speed.

3. Experience it twice (at least)

The big reason to listen more than once is that *you'll remember*

better what you hear. Research suggests that if you hear something only once, you forget 66 per cent of it within twenty-four
hours — nearly all of it within thirty days. Research also shows
that each time you relisten to information your chances of
remembering increase geometrically. The second reason to play
it again is that *you'll hear more*. Why? Because every time you
hear a good idea, your mind runs with it — analysing it, applying
it — all the while other good ideas are hitting 'dead air'. When
you find a particularly good tape programme, replay it until
you've squeezed out every last idea.

4. Stop the tape

When you hear a 'good' idea, use the pause button and decide
how you are going to put the idea to use. Write it down or
dictate it immediately. The physical act of stopping the tape
will reinforce your commitment to act on the information (it
also saves you from being distracted by what comes next). It
will help if, before you start listening, you make a mental note
of the goals and problems you have in the area the tape is
addressing — and keep them foremost in your mind. Submit
every idea, tip, and recommendation to your own usefulness
test to see what will work for you and what won't. That way
you're less likely to let good, usable ideas get away. And that
is why our constant refrain in this book is, it's not what you
know, but what you do with what you know that counts.

5. Use tapes for training

If you're a manager, one of your major responsibilities is to
keep your staff learning and growing on their jobs. Cassette
learning is an excellent way to leverage and supplement the
training programmes you already have, such as seminars, films,
and one-to-one training.

With cassettes you can provide a steady stream of quality
training at a fraction of the cost required to hire an outside
consultant or to send people to a seminar. Another advantage,
in addition to savings and convenience, is expertise. Cassettes
expose your staff to the most respected authorities in their fields.

There are lots of ways to make tape training work. One
is to play thirty minutes or so of a tape for your people in
a group. You can follow that up with a discussion of how you're

going to put what you learned to work. At CareerTrack, our managers often budget the last portion of their weekly department meetings for this kind of staff development.

Another way to use tapes for training is to assign a complete tape programme for your staff to listen to individually over a period of time, say a month. Then bring everyone together for a discussion. At CareerTrack we do this regularly. We've even named our monthly ritual: CareerTrack University. In fact, we also have a quiz. The purpose of the quiz is not so much to check up on people (although it does provide a bit of an incentive — nobody likes to flunk a quiz); it's more to reinforce the major themes or 'action items' of the programme. The advantage of this system is that everyone listens at their own convenience and can replay sections that are of particular value to them.

You can also take advantage of tapes in your company training by starting a company tape library so that people can borrow tapes for a few days (it's a perk they appreciate). Or route tapes as you would articles and books. Although tape training will never take the place of live or one-to-one training, it is an excellent way to cultivate an ongoing learning habit in your people. In other words, it's good management.

6. Reinforce the book with the tape

After reading a book, hearing it will produce new insights. When you're listening, your mind is freer to think, because you are not moving your eyes, concentrating on words, and turning pages. This makes it easier to focus on and absorb the author's message (especially if the author is also the narrator). Many classic business and career books are now being released in audiocassette format, some in a one-cassette condensed version and others in the full, unabridged, multicassette length. Now that it's possible, consider purchasing and *listening* to your old favourites.

7. 'Attend' by tape to save time

Have a schedule conflict and can't attend a seminar? Under pressure and can't take the time off to go to an important conference? Then get the tapes and 'attend' at your convenience. Budget one hour of listening time each day for a week (a typical commute time), and you'll have completed the average one-day seminar without ever having left your office. The same is true for conferences — most of the workshop sessions are recorded on cassettes and are available for sale. Why not stay home and simply purchase the tapes for the sessions which most interest you? Yes, you'll miss the opportunity to visit the exhibit stands and to socialize, but you'll also save three or four days and a lot of hassle.

8. Know what's available and where

Although audiocassette learning is a relatively new phenomenon, there are numerous sources of new and classic titles. Find out who are your local producers of audiocassette programmes and get your name on their mailing lists to receive announcements of new releases. Many traditional book publishers (even fiction publishers) are now publishing audiotape editions of their titles, and you can purchase them in most bookshops.

9. Give subliminal tapes a chance

When you play them it sounds like you're listening to classical music or waves at the beach. But there's a lot more here than meets the ear. Subliminal messages, messages that can be heard only by the subconscious mind, are being repeated over and over. The theory is that these messages go directly to the subconscious, without being judged or edited by the conscious mind, and are therefore more powerful. Think it's a load of rubbish? Not according to scientists. In study after study, it has been shown that subliminal tapes help people lose weight, become more productive, get better grades — the list goes on. Subliminal tapes are available on virtually any topic imaginable, including health, personal relationships, business success, and sport.

10. Discard bad tapes

There are a lot of bad tapes. Producing audiocassettes is a lot easier than producing a book, and a few people have got into the act to make some easy money. So if you run into a tape that hasn't aroused you within the first five minutes (whether because of boring material, a bad speaker, or poor technical quality), discard it. If you can, get your money back.

If you can't, make a mental note to boycott that publisher in the future. Too many cassette programmes are well worth your time and money for you to invest in the ones that aren't.

11. Keep an eye on video

Home video technology, once the domain only of Hollywood movies, is also becoming educational. There are still fewer self-help tapes available on videotape than on audiocassettes, but new products are reaching the market fast. Today videotape topics range from setting goals, to choosing wines, to meditation. And they're affordable. Most well-stocked video shops now also rent out instructional videotapes, too.

12. Listen!

That's right, listen. You can have six cassette players and three dozen tape packages, but if you don't put in a tape and concentrate, you won't learn much. Get committed to audiocassette learning by listening every time you get the chance. Make listening something you automatically do whenever you perform routine tasks. Programme yourself to insert a cassette and press 'play' as soon as you get into your car, start exercising, or whatever. You've got to listen to learn!

Network to Know and Be Known

Today's Way to Connect

In the network environment, rewards come by empowering others, not by climbing over them.
— JOHN NAISBITT, *MEGATRENDS*

In recent years hundreds of articles and books have been published on the subject of networking. Think it's a fad? Hardly. Networking is the old 'old-boy society' updated, reorganized, and *legitimized*.

We've all heard, 'It's not what you know, but who...'. This old proverb has never held more truth (though we would add the word 'just' before 'what you know' — brains still count, too). Nothing can move your career further and faster than having a base of associates positioned to support you in your goals. Conversely, few things feel better than using your talents to help others achieve their goals. Networking is one of the highest forms of collaboration.

Once considered informal, unstructured, and random, networking is now viewed as an essential — even scientific — way of developing professional relationships. Networking keeps you in touch by connecting you to new people and information. Once you get the hang of it, you will use networking every day to help verify data (and get the 'inside information' that is essential these days); solve problems; find employees, buyers, and suppliers; and get good advice and moral support — even a date on Saturday night! The possibilities are as endless as the range of human relationships.

Think of networking as the dynamic use of contacts. It can open up a world of opportunities for you, yet it's very simple. Follow these twelve guidelines, and you'll be tapping the power of networking before you know it.

THE HOW-TO-DO-ITS

1. Make networking a high priority

As we said in Success Shortcut 21, the qualities that turn a wish into a goal are numbers and dates. Use this quantification principle to guide you in networking as well. For instance, consider this goal: In the next twelve months I will establish relationships with five new social contacts, three new supplier sources, two friendly competitors, and one industry luminary. Now that sounds like a goal that will become a reality! Integrate networking into your monthly goal-setting exercise and you will enjoy its benefits much sooner. Don't let your network develop just as a by-product of doing business; approach it actively.

2. Organize your current network

Yes, you already have one. It's your phone index, address book, business cards, and correspondence files. Take the time to organize these resources. It's good to organize your network in one place, perhaps separating it into your personal and professional relationships (inasmuch as they're possible to keep separate these days). Keep it flexible and expandable. Many people find a card index ideal; others store their networks in sophisticated computer data bases.

3. Get yourself out there

Go to conferences, seminars, workshops, special events — anyplace where you can meet people with similar interests. Trade associations and clubs (for instance, the Chamber of Commerce and Rotary Club) enable you to get to know people and thereby expand your network. Be a player. In just about every large city today there are organizations set up for the express purpose of networking. Check them out and become part of the ones that meet your needs and feel right to you.

4. Advertise yourself

A key step in networking is to *raise your visibility*. You can do this by writing articles in trade journals, speaking before

groups, holding office in your clubs, or becoming the spokesperson for your department or work team. Become the recognized authority on something — someone worth getting to know.
These days, actively making a name for yourself is considered
OK. What's more, if you're serious about getting ahead, it's
necessary.

5. Make the first contact

As your mother used to say, 'This is no time to be shy'. Whether
it's a business situation or a social situation, when you see
someone you might like to have in your network, take the risk
and introduce yourself. Go into the conversation with an open-
ended attitude; make it your business to find out as much as
you can about the other person, and you'll probably find a willing partner. Just as the longest journey begins with the first
step, achieving a goal often begins with the first contact.

6. Be a promoter of others

Regularly talk to the people in your network. When you
encounter someone with a need, offer to share a contact. It
doesn't have to be a 'direct hit' — a friend of a friend might
be just right. You will do both parties a favour of fulfilling
the needs of one while giving an opportunity to another.

7. Remember the key word: Ask

Asking questions is the 'activator' in networking. For example,
to expand your network ask current contacts, 'Who do you
know who could...?' To gain information ask, 'Do you know
where I could find...?' It has been said that you get the answer
you need to any question in five calls or less. In our experience
it can usually be done in three. The next time you're faced
with a tough new problem and you don't know where to begin,
remember that.

8. Keep in touch

How? By regularly writing letters and cards; sending articles
of interest; phonecalls; or having lunch, dinner, or a squash
game after work. Here's a novel idea: start a 'What's New with
me Newsletter' and send it monthly to your family, friends,
and associates. A handwritten message in the corner will keep

it personal. However you choose to keep in touch, remember these three words: short, chatty, and frequent. A note is as good as a letter; lunch as good as dinner. People don't remember how extensive the contact was — just that you made it.

9. Network with competitors

We're serious! There are many issues you can discuss with your competitors without giving away secrets or hurting your competitive position. Even better, there are many ways you can *mutually benefit* by comparing your common challenges. Make it a point to develop a 'friendly competitor' relationship with others in your industry. In networking you get value by giving value.

10. Remember people's special days

There's no better way to build rapport than to remember people on birthdays, anniversaries, and big events. Send a simple card, flowers, balloons. Again, the message is less important than the contact itself. Set up a calendar of special days and check it weekly. Buy a supply of cards and stationery. If you're really organized you can write a year's worth of cards in one evening. Or give your local florist a list of people, dates, and occasions, and have him or her send flowers automatically. You're a busy person, but with some clever work you'll remember everyone who's important to you.

11. Say thanks

Here's another small investment with a big return. Reinforce your network by taking the time to thank the people who help you. Did a friend of a friend give you some information you needed? Did a customer refer a new customer to you? Jot them a quick note of thanks. This reinforcement will strengthen the bond and encourage them to think of you in the future. (Written thank-yous are particularly important in sales, where networked referrals can translate into cold, hard cash.)

12. Sell networking to others

Your network is stronger if the people in it have active networks of their own. Talk it over! Encourage your associates to network both inside and outside your company. Share your enthusiasm for networking, and everyone will profit by it. And remember: by promoting an environment of listening, caring, and helping, you have made the process of doing business not only more efficient but also more fun.

Get Your Next Salary Rise and Promotion

How High Can You Go?

*What's the matter? Don't you believe
in your own future?*
— BEN STEIN, *DREEMZ*

In business there are generally only two directions in which you can go: up or out. Up is preferred. Whether it's in the form of more money, a better office, or a higher title, most people need regular evidence that they are growing. Likewise, a company needs regular evidence that its people are growing. In terms of professional success, salary rises and promotions are how we mark this.

But salary increases and promotions have more than symbolic importance. The fact is, the best benefits are quite substantive. Look at money, for instance: the more you have, the more stuff you can buy! And *that's* not even the best part.

The *best* part is that the higher you move in your organization, the more power you have. That means power to change things, to express youself, to colour your organization to reflect your own goals and values.

Don't tell anyone this, but in many ways life is easier at the top. You're more respected; you're more in control. The assignments are more glamorous and challenging. You associate with people who are more successful and more fun to be around (and make no mistake about it, successful people are happier than unsuccessful people).

Another way to look at the benefits of salary rises and promotions is to consider the consequence of not growing: stagnation. Are you feeling the moss beginning to grow around the edges of your career? If so, a salary rise and promotion will give you the shot in the arm you need to feel challenged and enthusiastic again.

At the risk of bursting the bubble, allow us to make one final point: the higher you are promoted, the harder it is to be promoted even higher. This is unfortunate, but inescapably true (after all, there are fewer high-level jobs than low-level jobs). Today, especially, more and more qualified people are competing for fewer and fewer plum jobs. That means the people who get ahead are the ones who not only know how to *do the job*, but also know how to *win the job*. This chapter will show you what it takes to gain a promotion. It just may make the difference in how high *you* can go.

THE HOW-TO-DO-ITS

1. Make sure you want it

And deserve it. Ultimately the only way to get ahead in business is to *become more valuable* (salary rises and promotions should never be asked for — or given — because of need). It's also important to communicate your increased value to your superiors, in their language. So ask yourself: Are you really ready to move up a rung? Are you committed to making it happen?

2. Do more, much more

As we said in Success Shortcut 2, consider your job description the foundation of your responsibilities, not the boundary (and if you don't have an accurate job description, write your own and get your manager's approval). Look for for new ways to contribute to your company. Volunteer for assignments (particularly the ones no one else wants). Help your boss in ways he or she doesn't expect — few things in business are more powerful than giving people more than they bargained for.

3. Dress 'up'

Remember the saying, 'Dress for the job you want, not for the job you have'. Make it easy for the people responsible for promoting you to visualize you in your new job. It's an old maxim that people shouldn't. But they do. In fact, many studies have shown that people react to others in radically different ways depending on their dress and personal grooming. Make sure you are getting the reactions that support your goals. Another benefit of dressing 'up' is that you generally feel better and perform better, too. Your appearance is closely connected to your self-image, and by looking the part you'll convince yourself you deserve a salary rise and a promotion, too!

4. Be a self-appointed problem-solver

This is *the* key skill for upper-level positions. A good way to improve your problem-solving ability is to require yourself to report to your boss, not just problems, but also options and recommendations. This is the 'completed staff work' principle again (see Success Shortcut 2). If your recommendation is correct (and you may come up with a solution your boss would not have thought of), it's a feather in your cap. If you're wrong, you can ask your boss to show you where you went off the track, thereby improving your problem-solving capabilities for the future. This simple principle also works in managing staff. When you require them to come to you, not only with problems, but also with options and recommendations, you help them grow. (You also get better solutions than you may have come up with on your own.)

5. Stand in the spotlight

Remember, it's not enough to do a good job; *you must be seen doing a good job.* Keep people tuned in to what you're doing. You can do this by writing memo updates on your projects (with copies to all affected parties), being your department's or group's spokesperson, volunteering for high-visibility projects, writing for the company newsletter, and asking to be invited to meetings where you can make a contribution. Think about how you can increase your profile in your company. (Success Shortcut 22 will get you started.)

6. Read, write, talk, and listen — better

The higher you go, the more important communication skills become. High-level people in most organizations spend very little time on the technical aspects of tasks. They spend their time on the people aspects, and that means communicating. To reach the top you must be able to get other people to listen to you, face-to-face, in meetings, on the phone, in front of audiences. You must also be able to *receive* communication from other people, by listening skilfully, getting people to relax and open up, spotting and eliminating misunderstandings, and reading body language.

Ask yourself which communication skill you most need to improve: one-to-one communication, listening, writing, making presentations? We have included in this book a Success Shortcut for each of these critical skills. You'll get the best results if you concentrate on one at a time.

7. Know your organization inside out

In most companies gaining a working knowledge of how the organization functions as a whole is not a big part of your training; it's something you must take charge of yourself. The rewards are enormous. After all, the more you know about how other departments operate, the better you can work with them. Also, you're better positioned and qualified to take advantage of any internal transfers that might become available. Another aspect of your company it pays to know inside out is the *informal* power structure. Who's in the 'in crowd'? Which people exercise power far beyond their job titles? Very few organizations operate in accordance with their organizational charts. Find out where the real power lies in your company, and align yourself with it.

8. Do your salary homework

Find out what others in your field are earning to see if your current salary is in line. You might find that you could be earning more elsewhere. If so, you may want to let your boss know about it (chances are he or she isn't aware of the salary levels elsewhere). Or, of course, you may want to go after the higher-paying job (after telling your boss, you may not have a choice). On the other hand, you might find you are well paid in your current position. If so, now is the time to consider a promotion that would put you in a higher earning category.

Knowing what he was worth on the open market helped Jeff engineer a doubling of his salary. It was in his first job, as the copywriter at a medium-sized advertising agency. About a year into the job Jeff won a major advertising award. He was thrilled; and everyone was proud of him, especially his boss.

The next afternoon Jeff received a call from a fairly well-known advertising agency — the big time! They wanted to talk about the possibility of his going to work for them.

Jeff had no intention of working for this company. For one thing, he was loyal to his current company, a good agency with good people who had given him every chance in the world. Still, he felt he owed it to himself to check out the option. Although it was only remotely conceivable that this new company would make him an offer he couldn't refuse, Jeff was still eager to talk. His primary goal was simply to find out what he was worth on the open market — an important thing to know.

The day of the meeting, Jeff was in great form. Since he really wanted to find out how much he could make them want him, he prepared an excellent presentation. But since he didn't really want the job, he was freed of the debilitating anxiety that often accompanies job interviews. It worked. Within their first hour together, the company had offered Jeff a starting salary close to double what he was making at his own firm. He told them, with all the nonchalance he could muster, that he would think about it.

Think about it was all he could do for the next several days. Luckily the bout of introspection didn't keep Jeff from functioning. He knew he wanted to take things one step further — he had to find out if his boss thought he was worth as much as the other company.

Jeff met with his boss and told him everything that had happened: who had offered him a job and how much they'd offered, and that in the interest of his career he felt he had to consider it. Jeff said he would stay if the company would match the other offer; otherwise, he would complete the projects at hand and leave.

His boss didn't say yes. In fact, for a few long moments he didn't say anything at all. His coop had been raided, there was mutiny brewing, and he had to regroup. Finally he said simply that he appreciated Jeff's position but he would have to think about it.

Fair enough. Jeff couldn't blame him for wanting to think. Besides, he was pretty sure the answer would be yes. And it was. The next morning as they passed each other in the hall, his boss grabbed Jeff by the arm. 'OK, I'll match it,' he said.

'We've got a lot of work to do around here'. That was all that was ever said about it between them. It's nice to know your worth on the open market.

9. Help them justify it

This is where a lot of otherwise competent professionals fall down. They expect their bosses to remember every contribution they've made (and when their bosses don't, they complain that 'nobody appreciates me'). Take personal responsibility for making sure the people who count know what you've contributed. Start a 'win file', in which you keep track of your accomplishments. Document how you've exceeded your job description (helped out another department, for example), cut costs, increased productivity, or improved the work environment. You can even create material for your win file by asking people who praise you if they wouldn't mind writing a quick note of thanks so you can show your boss. Then make sure you give your boss your win file *at least a week before your performance evaluation*, so he or she can use the information in deciding how much to increase your salary. If you wait and present it after your boss has made his or her decision (and got approval and done all the paperwork, etc.), you're putting your boss in the position of having to change a decision, instead of making an informed decision from the outset. Trust us; if handled properly, preparing a win file can be one of your wisest investments in yourself.

10. Let them know you want it

Ask for it, but don't come on too strong. If you're turned down, do ask for reasons, but be sure you ask in the spirit of learning rather than the spirit of argument. Also, use your judgement as to your organization's current outlook (is your company going through lean or robust times?). And consider taking no for an answer. (Note: Play by the rules. Don't forget to respect the chain of command. If you appear to be more interested in your own success than that of your team or company, people will be motivated to resist you rather than support you.)

11. Make a kinetic commitment

In other words, set your salary rise and promotion goals right now *on paper*. Write down your objectives, achievement strategies, measurement standards, and timetable. Keep an ongoing log of all your accomplishments and contributions. Spend ten minutes a week updating it. Should you send a copy to your boss? Good idea!

12. Raise those below you

If you manage people, you must be committed to raising and promoting them. The quickest way to get ahead is by having a staff of superstars. If you feel threatened, figure out why, because a star employee can only make you look good. If you find yourself managing true superstars whose talents surpass yours, let them pass you by. If they are genuinely more talented, you will gain far more respect if you don't hold them back. Concentrate on what you do best, and let them pursue their own goals. Having subordinates pass you by may be a bitter pill to swallow, but it's far better than driving outstanding employees away because you put your own interests ahead of your organization's.

To Become an Expert

As you read *CareerTracking*, you undoubtedly came across
topics that struck a nerve. Perhaps you recognized areas you
need to improve or skills that are particularly important in
your profession. If so, the following resources can help you
become an expert.

As we've said, the two of us read, watch, or listen to most
of the material that exists on the subject of success. It's our
business. We once heard that if you read three good books on
a given subject, you will be one of the world's authorities on
it. Whether or not that is actually true, it makes a good point.

In this section we've pulled together the best of literally
hundreds of books. By following our recommendations below
you'll be spared a lot of sources that might otherwise waste
your time (or, worse, give you bad information).

To make it easy for you to find what you need, we've grouped
the resources into three sections, which correspond generally
with the three main themes of the book.

Success Shortcuts 1-10

SUCCESS WITH YOURSELF

*Every professional has too much to do. Today that's a fact. The
challenge is to make more of an impact with less effort. The
following resources will help you do just that.*

BOOKS

Arnold, John. *The Art of Decision-Making*. New York:
AMACOM, 1978
**The seven building blocks of decision-making and how
to apply them to any decision you make.**

Bandler, Richard, and John Grinder. *Frogs into Princes*. Moab,
UT: Real People Press, 1979.
**The first and most complete presentation of
neurolinguistic programming, by the originators of
the science.**

Bates, Jefferson. *Dictating Effectively*. Washington, DC:
Acropolis Books, 1986.
**How to overcome 'dictaphobia' and double your
productivity with dictation.**

Biss, Edwin C. *Doing It Now*. London: Macdonald, 1983.
Short question-and-answer format will make sure you don't put off reading it!

Burka, Jane and Lenora Yuen. *Procrastination*. Reading, MA: Addison–Wesley, 1985.
A psychological approach, this book shows you how to overcome procrastination by facing the fears that may be holding you back.

Burns, David D. *Feeling Good: The New Mood Therapy*. New York: William Morrow and Co., 1980.
Use the principles of cognitive therapy to change the way you think and thereby change your moods.

Cutler, Wade E. *Triple Your Reading Speed*. New York: Arco Publishing Inc., 1970.
Does just what it says.

Dyer, Wayne. *Your Erroneous Zones*. London Sphere, 1977.
One of our all-time favourite self-actualization books. It shows you how to cut through a lifetime of emotional red tape.

Erickson, Steve M. *Management Tools for Everyone*. New York: Petrocelli Books, 1981.
From decisions trees to Gantt charts to force field analysis, this book lays out 20 classic tools of management.

Gawain, Shakti. *Creative Visualization*. New York: Bantam Books, 1978.
Through easy-to-follow exercises, meditations, and affirmations, you'll learn to use mental energy to make your positive ideas a reality.

Hill, Napoleon. *Think and Grow Rich*. New York: Fawcett Crest, 1983.
A classic. This book proves that 'whatever the mind can conceive and believe, it can achieve'.

Lakein, Alan. *How to Get Control of Your Time and Your Life*. Aldershot, Gower, 1984.
One of the two bestselling books ever written on how to manage your personal and business time.

Mackenzie, R. Alex. *The Time Trap*. New York: McGraw-Hill, 1972.
This is the other one. A classic.

Maltz, Maxwell. *Psychocybernetics*. 2nd edn. Wellingborough: Thorsons, 1969.
A new way to get more living out of life by acquiring the habit of happiness.

Peters, Tom, and Nancy Austin. *A Passion for Excellence*. London: Collins, 1985.
Gives the 'how-to-do-its' of the 'management excellence' revolution. A MUST FOR MANAGERS.

Tubesing, Donald A. *Kicking Your Stress Habits*. Duluth, MN: Whole Person Associates, 1981.
A do-it-yourself guide to coping with stress. Filled with fun and enlightening exercises.

Von Oech, Roger. *A Whack on the Side of the Head*. London: Angus and Roberston, 1983.
A humorous and entertaining look at the ten blocks that prevent you from being innovative — and how to overcome them.

Wonder, Jacquelyn, and Priscilla Donovan. *Whole Brain Thinking*. New York: William Morrow and Co., 1984.
A terrific introduction to left brain/right brain theory, and how to use it to increase your mental powers.

Success Shortcuts 11–20

SUCCESS WITH PEOPLE

As we noted on page 4 in our Introduction's 'core beliefs', all business is people business. To get to the top you need to know how to get results with people. These resources will make it a lot easier.

BOOKS

Bates, Jefferson. *Writing with Precision*. Washington, DC: Acropolis Books, 1978.
The simple way to write so that you cannot possibly be misunderstood.

Bennis, Warren and Burt Nanus. *Leaders: Strategies for Taking Charge*. New York: Harper and Row Publishers, 1985.
Filled with the personal observations of sixty contem-

porary CEOs, this book describes, in an engaging and thought-provoking manner, the four keys to effective leadership.

Blanchard, Kenneth, and Spencer Johnson. *The One Minute Manager*. London: Collins, 1983.
You still haven't read it? Then get moving . . . this book is as good as its hype.

Blanchard, Kenneth, Patricia Zigarmi and Drea Zigarmi. *Leadership and the One Minute Manager*. London: Fontana, 1987.
From the One Minute library, this book shows how to change your management style for different people and situations.

Bramson, Robert. *Coping with Difficult People*. Garden City, NY: Anchor Press, 1981.
The classic book for dealing with all the people who make you want to scream.

Burley–Allen, Madelyn. *Listening, the Forgotten Skill*. New York: John Wiley and Sons, 1982.
An engaging book that actively involves you through its exercises, drawings, and examples.

Carlzon, Jan. *Moments of Truth*. Cambridge, MA: Ballinger Publishing Co., 1987.
Many companies give lip service to 'putting the customer first', but Jan Carlzon put it into practice. Learn how he transformed his company by structuring it around that premise.

Cohen, Herb. *You Can Negotiate Anything*. Don Mills, ON: Lyle Stuart Inc., 1980.
Specific tactics for dealing with everyone from your boss to your spouse to your department store to your banker.

Coplin, William D., and Michael K. O'Leary. *Power Persuasion*. Reading, MA: Addison–Wesley, 1985.
A sure-fire system to get ahead in business.

Doyle, Michael and David Strauss. *How to Make Meetings Work*. New York: The Berkley Publishing Group, 1976.
Whether you're the meeting leader or the meeting goer, use the Interaction Method to stop wasting time and get things done fast.

Geneen, Harold, with Alvin Moscow. *Managing*. Aldershot: Gower, 1986.

When Harold Geneen took over ITT, sales were $766 million. When he stepped down, sales were $22 billion. His (sometimes unconventional) views are presented here along with the experiences that shaped them.

Grove, Andrew S. *High Output Management*. London: Pan Books, 1985.

A manager's output is measured by the output of the people he or she supervises or influences. Stimulate that output by concentrating on the high-leverage activities that will have the strongest influence over a long period of time.

Harris, Thomas A. *I'm OK, You're OK*. London: Pan Books, 1973.

Another self-help classic. Harris lays out the principles of transactional analysis that can dramatically improve your relationships.

Hyatt, Carole, and Linda Gottlieb. *When Smart People Fail*. New York: Simon & Schuster, 1987.

Learn how defeats are 'not only survivable, but can be tools for renewed success'.

Linver, Sandy. *Speak and Get Results*. New York: Summit Books, 1983.

A complete guide to speeches and presentations that will work in any situation.

McCormack, Mark H. *What They Don't Teach You At Harvard Business School*. London: Collins, 1984.

Subtitled 'Notes From a Street Smart Executive', this book pulls no punches about how negotiations really happen at the top levels of business.

Montgomery, Robert L. *Listening Made Easy*. New York: AMACOM, 1981.

The barriers to effective listening are everywhere — yet the art of listening is seldom taught anywhere. Here's one place where you can learn the key concepts.

Reimold, Cheryl. *How to Write a Million Dollar Memo*. New York: Dell Publishing Co., 1984.

The title says it all. This book describes techniques

that will help your memos get the results you want.

Steinmetz, Lawrence. *The Art and Skill of Delegation.* Reading, MA: Addison–Wesley, 1976.

The best guidebook on how to give work away.

Wells, Theodora. *Keeping Your Cool Under Fire.* New York: McGraw–Hill Book Co., 1980.

How to communicate non-defensively with confidence and composure in the toughest situations.

Wilder, Lilyan. *Professional Speaking.* New York: Simon & Schuster, 1986.

How to get your message across and sound your best — with a special section on 'Speaking Up and Speaking Out' in selling, in discussions with superiors, and when under pressure.

Zinsser, William. *On Writing Well.* New York: Harper & Row Publishers Inc., 1985.

An informal guide to writing non-fiction, with sections on sexist language, humour, and building unity.

Success Shortcuts 21–26

SUCCESS IN YOUR CAREER

These days managing your career is a job in itself. The following resources will give you a clearer view of where you are in your career, what your greatest challenges are, and what your next moves should be.

BOOKS

Bolles, Richard. *What Color Is Your Parachute?* Berkeley, CA: Ten Speed Press, 1988.

Updated annually, this is a practical manual for discovering the skills you enjoy most, what job to use them in, and who has the power to employ you.

Calano, James, and Jeff Salzman. *Real World 101.* New York: Warner Books, 1984.

The basics of how to look, think, and act like a promotable achiever. Perfect for new professionals *and* those who want a refresher.

Campbell, David. *If you don't know where you're going you'll probably end up somewhere else.* Allen, TX: Argus Communications, 1974.
Goal-setting at its best.

Ferguson, Marilyn. *The Aquarian Conspiracy.* London: Routledge and Kegan Paul, 1981.
Fascinating account of a loose network of thousands of people who are dedicated to furthering human potential.

Glasser, William. *Positive Addiction.* New York: Harper & Row, 1976.
How to get hooked on things that are good for you.

Harragan, Betty. *Games Mother Never Taught You.* New York: Warner Books, 1978.
Subtitled 'Corporate Gamesmanship for Women', this is a classic, a must-read for women with high career goals.

Hudson, Diane, and Jan Simon, editors. Chapters by CareerTrack's ten top women trainers. *Reach Your Career Dreams.* Boulder, CO: CareerTrack Publications Inc., 1986.
Network to get known, project a high profile, get (or advance) your college degree without classes — these are three of the twelve topics covered in this handbook for professional women.

Kahn, Michael. *Power!* New York: Random House, 1985.
From power plays to power symbols — how to get power and use it. Enjoy, but don't take it too seriously.

Kushner, Harold. *When All You Ever Wanted Isn't Enough.* London: Pan Books, 1987.
An entertaining, inspiring guide to finding meaning in life and determining what you really want.

Naisbitt, John. *Megatrends.* London: Macdonald, 1982.
A landmark book; Naisbitt labels networking as one of the ten megatrends transforming our lives.

Schwimmmer, Lawrence D. *Winning Your Next Promotion in One Year (or Less!).* New York: Harper & Row, 1986.
How to set and execute a one-year (or less) plan for promotion.

Welch, Mary Scott. *Networking.* New York: Warner Books, 1981.
Highly readable, practical guide to the dos and don'ts

of networking. It even has a nationwide networking directory.

Do Something Now

It's not what you know . . .

This concludes the twenty-six Success Shortcuts, techniques which have been proven effective by the hundreds of thousands of people we train in our seminars every year.

These skills can create more success in your life, too. All you have to do is remember one thing (dare we say it one more time?): *It's not what you know, it's what you do with what you know that counts.* That means putting these ideas to work, relentlessly.

To assist you in that noble task, we have prepared an action plan (see page 269). We suggest you copy this action plan, then take the time to look through the book again. Skim all the how-to-do-it pointers, reread any points or chapters which you think deserve special attention, and reflect on how the information relates to your own situation. As you do this, write down on your action plan the specific actions you are going to take as a result of your new knowledge. Here are a few tricks to make the process even more effective.

Don't try to write down every last idea that you can possibly squeeze from the material, and don't worry about creating a masterpiece. That's too big a job, and you'll give up after the first chapter — if you ever start at all. Skim and write down only the ideas that come to you easily. The whole process shouldn't take more than an hour, but it will give you enough ideas to keep you busy for the next six months.

Pick the two or three best ideas and do something with them immediately. Write an affirmation, add another point to your goal-setting sheet (from Success Shortcut 21), delegate one aspect of it — but do something right away! Research shows that if you use an idea within twenty-four hours of hearing it, you are more likely to integrate it permanently. One small, immediate initiative is worth a thousand grandiose plans you never got around to.

That's about it. Thanks for reading our book and giving our ideas a fair try. If you maintain your enthusiasm, commitment, and activist approach, your career will move far and fast. Because *CareerTracking* works — especially in the long run.

MY ACTION PLAN

Don't let a good idea get away!

Research shows that if you use an idea within twenty-four hours of being exposed to it, you are more likely to integrate it permanently. So when you read something in *CareerTracking* that you'd like to use, *write it down on this page immediately* (we suggest you use a photocopy). Then take it back to your workplace and hang it where you can't miss it. That way you can put your action plan into action!

The Actions I'll Take	I'll Get Started By	I'll Finish By
1.		
2.		
3.		
4.		
5.		
6.		
7.		
8.		
9.		
10.